True Faith

True Faith

by
John MacArthur, Jr.

A catalog of all materials can be obtained by writing to:

Word of Grace Communications
P.O. Box 4000
Panorama City, CA 91412

All Scripture quotations, unless noted otherwise, are from the *New Scofield Reference Bible*, King James Version. Copyright © 1967 by Oxford University Press, Inc. Reprinted by permission.

Library of Congress Cataloging in Publication Data

MacArthur, John, 1939-
    True faith / by John MacArthur, Jr.
       p.   cm. — (John MacArthur's Bible studies)
    ISBN 0-8024-5381-3
    1. Bible. N.T. James I, 19-II, 26—Criticism, interpretation, etc. 2. Faith—Biblical teaching. I. Title. II. Series: MacArthur, John, 1939-   Bible studies.
    BS2785.6.F3M33   1989
227'.9107—dc19   89-2990
                                                            CIP

1 2 3 4 5 6 Printing/LC/Year 93 92 91 90 89

Printed in the United States of America

Contents

These Bible studies are taken from messages delivered by Pastor-Teacher John MacArthur, Jr., at Grace Community Church in Panorama City, California. These messages have been combined into an 8-tape album entitled *True Faith*. You may purchase this series either in an attractive vinyl cassette album or as individual cassettes. To purchase these tapes, request the album *True Faith*, or ask for the tapes by their individual GC numbers. Please consult the current price list; then, send your order, making your check payable to:

WORD OF GRACE COMMUNICATIONS
P.O. Box 4000
Panorama City, CA 91412

Or call the following toll-free number:
1-800-55-GRACE

1
The Belief That Behaves—Part 1

Outline

Introduction
A. The Attitude of Faith
    1. Psalm 119:1
    2. Psalm 119:10
    3. Psalm 119:14
B. The Obedience of Faith
    1. As evidenced in Psalm 119
    2. As evidenced in Psalm 1
    3. As evidenced in the writings of John
      a) 3 John 11
      b) 1 John 2:24
    4. As evidenced in the epistle of James

Lesson
I. A Proper Reception of the Word (vv. 19-21)
A. A Willingness to Receive the Word with Submission (vv. 19-20)
    1. Unbelievers resist the truth
      a) 2 Timothy 3:8
      b) 2 Timothy 4:14-15
    2. Believers submit to the truth
      a) A compassionate exhortation (v. 19*a*)
        (1) "My beloved brothers"
        (2) "This you know"
      b) A careful exposition (vv. 19*b*-20)
        (1) "Swift to hear"
          (*a*) What it does not mean
          (*b*) What it does mean

      (2) "Slow to speak"
         (*a*) Defined
            i) What it does not mean
            ii) What it does mean
         (*b*) Demonstrated
            i) James 3:1-2
            ii) 1 Timothy 3:6
            iii) 1 Timothy 5:22
            iv) Ezekiel 3:17; 33:6-7
            v) Hebrews 13:17
         (*c*) Described
            i) James 1:26
            ii) James 3:1
            iii) James 4:6-12
            iv) James 5:9
      (3) "Slow to wrath"
         (*a*) Defined
         (*b*) Demonstrated
            i) James 4:1-3
            ii) Galatians 4:16
         (*c*) Defended
  B. A Willingness to Receive the Word with Purity (v. 21*a*)
    1. The principle
    2. The particulars
      a) The action
        (1) Ephesians 4:22
        (2) Colossians 3:8
        (3) Hebrews 12:1
        (4) 1 Peter 2:1-2
      b) The evil
    3. The pattern
  C. A Willingness to Receive the Word with Humility (v. 21*b*)
    1. How do we receive it?
    2. What do we receive?
    3. Why do we receive it?
      a) Romans 13:11
      b) Romans 1:16
      c) Hebrews 4:12
Conclusion

Introduction

A. The Attitude of Faith

The desire of a believer is to pattern his life after the Word of God.

1. Psalm 119:1—"Blessed are the undefiled in the way, who walk in the law of the Lord."

2. Psalm 119:10—"With my whole heart have I sought thee; oh, let me not wander from thy commandments."

3. Psalm 119:14—"I have rejoiced in the way of thy testimonies, as much as in all riches."

The desire of an unbeliever is to avoid the Word of God. Psalm 119:155 says, "Salvation is far from the wicked; for they seek not thy statutes." Jeremiah 6:16 says, "Thus saith the Lord, Stand in the ways, and see, and ask for the old paths, where is the good way, and walk in it, and ye shall find rest for your souls. But they said, We will not walk in it."

B. The Obedience of Faith

1. As evidenced in Psalm 119

   a) Psalm 119:130—"The entrance of thy words giveth light; it giveth understanding unto the simple."

   b) Psalm 119:161—"My heart standeth in awe of thy word."

   c) Psalm 119:70—"I delight in thy law."

   d) Psalm 119:46—"I will speak of thy testimonies also before kings, and will not be ashamed."

   e) Psalm 119:81—"I hope in thy word."

   f) Psalm 119:45—"I seek thy precepts."

g) Psalm 119:5—"Oh, that my ways were directed to keep thy statutes!"

h) Psalm 119:33—"Teach me, O Lord, the way of thy statutes, and I shall keep it unto the end."

i) Psalm 119:35—"Make me to go in the path of thy commandments; for therein do I delight."

j) Psalm 119:133—"Order my steps in thy word, and let not any iniquity have dominion over me."

k) Psalm 119:10—"With my whole heart have I sought thee; oh, let me not wander from thy commandments."

l) Psalm 119:36-37—"Incline my heart unto thy testimonies, and not to covetousness. Turn away mine eyes from beholding vanity, and revive thou me in thy way."

Two key verses of Psalm 119 are verse 112—"I have inclined mine heart to perform thy statutes always, even unto the end"—and verse 97—"Oh, how I love thy law! It is my meditation all the day."

2. As evidenced in Psalm 1

He who possesses saving faith is described in Psalm 1:2 as one whose "delight is in the law of the Lord; and in his law doth he meditate day and night." The godly are those who love the Word of God and long to follow it. Their highest joy, greatest treasure, and deepest delight is obeying God's law.

One's attitude toward Scripture is a test of the nature of his faith. He who possesses true saving faith will demonstrate a compelling desire to hear and obey the Word of God.

3. As evidenced in the writings of John

   a) 3 John 11—"Beloved, follow not that which is evil, but that which is good. He that doeth good is of God, but he that doeth evil hath not seen God." Your response to the Word of God indicates the genuineness of your faith.

   b) 1 John 2:24—"Let that, therefore, abide in you which ye have heard from the beginning. If that which ye have heard from the beginning shall remain in you, ye also shall continue in the Son, and in the Father." The reality of saving faith and its continuity is linked to a life of obedience.

4. As evidenced in the epistle of James

   Throughout his epistle, James provides us with tests for living faith—tests by which you can measure the reality of your faith. The first test is the test of trials. How you respond to trials is an indicator of whether your faith is real or not. The second test is how you respond to temptation. The third test is how you respond to the Word of God.

   How a person responds to trials and temptations is a monitor that measures his faith. How a person responds to the Word of God is equally a monitor. How you listen to, react to, desire, and obey the Word reveals the nature of your faith and gives—in a sense—your spiritual temperature.

   God's Word is the originator of the new birth and the agent of transformation (v. 18). It is the Word of truth—the incorruptible seed 1 Peter 1:23 talks about. The Word of truth is present at the beginning of our spiritual life, and it becomes the focal point for the rest of our spiritual existence. As it was the generating power of our new birth, so it is the continuing power of our new life. Just as the Word is the power that brings about the new birth, it is also the power that feeds the new believer. That's why Peter said, "As newborn babes, desire the pure milk of the word, that ye may grow by it" (1 Pet. 2:2).

Having been born again by the Word, we become its pupils. Our heart's desire is to listen to it, learn from it, and respond to it—just as a baby desires milk. You don't have to teach a baby to like milk or to want to eat. The sensation of hunger is a lifelong occurrence.

The same is true of a believer. He has a normal spiritual appetite toward the things of God. If such an appetite is present—even though the person doesn't always appear hungry—it indicates that the new birth has taken place. If such an appetite is not present, it indicates that the new birth has not taken place.

James makes two major points in regard to saving faith. Saving faith is marked by a proper reception of the Word and a proper reaction to the Word.

Lesson

I. A PROPER RECEPTION OF THE WORD (vv. 19-21)

"Wherefore, my beloved brethren, let every man be swift to hear, slow to speak, slow to wrath; for the wrath of man worketh not the righteousness of God. Wherefore, put away all filthiness and overflowing of wickedness, and receive with meekness the engrafted word, which is able to save your souls."

The key word is "receive." A true believer receives the Word—His dial is tuned to the frequency of God's Word. He desires God's message, and he wants to obey what God says. When he is disobedient he feels himself caught in a terrible vise. Yet in his deepest self he longs to obey, not disobey.

In Mark 4:24 Jesus says, "Take heed *what* ye hear" (emphasis added). In Luke 8:18 He says, "Take heed . . . *how* ye hear" (emphasis added). The true believer looks at the "what" (the content) and the "how" (the intensity with which he responds to the Word of God).

Jesus illustrates that principle in the parable of the soils in Matthew 13. Some people hear the Word, and some do not. In verse 16 Jesus says, "Blessed are your eyes, for they see; and your ears, for they hear." The disciples were blessed to understand what had been hidden from the unbelieving (Matt. 11:25). You hear and understand when your faith is real and when you have made a connection with the living God. Within that connection is an outpouring of love, life, and power that makes you receptive to the Word of God.

Such a response to the Word identifies us as true believers—but at the same time we need to cultivate our receptivity. We can't sit back and wait for it to happen. It takes commitment to realize the fullness of being true receivers of God's Word.

According to James, a right response to the Word involves three things: willingness to receive the Word with submission, purity, and humility.

A. A Willingness to Receive the Word with Submission (vv. 19-20)

"Wherefore, my beloved brethren, let every man be swift to hear, slow to speak, slow to wrath; for the wrath of man worketh not the righteousness of God."

1. Unbelievers resist the truth

Unbelievers do not submit to the Word of God. It may irritate, aggravate, or exacerbate their predisposition against the things of God, but they won't willingly submit to it.

a) 2 Timothy 3:8—Ungodly people resist the truth. The Greek verb translated "resist" (*anthistēmi*) means to stand against the truth.

b) 2 Timothy 4:14-15—Paul said, "Alexander, the coppersmith, did me much evil; the Lord reward him according to his works, of whom do thou beware also; for he hath greatly withstood our words." Alexander the coppersmith is a typical example of an unbeliever in opposition to the Word of God. He's like the rocky soil described in Matthew 13 (vv. 5-6, 20-21). He hears for a while, but shuts out the message when he realizes there's a price to pay. An unbeliever is also like the weedy soil (vv. 7, 22)—he listens a little while. But if he has to give up the things of this world, or is overcome by the cares of this age and the deceitfulness of riches, he no longer desires to hear.

2. Believers submit to the truth

   a) A compassionate exhortation (v. 19*a*)

   (1) "My beloved brethren"

   James was being sensitive, concerned, compassionate, and loving as he exhorted his people. He called them his "beloved brethren"—a familiar phrase repeated throughout his epistle (v. 16), along with "my brethren" (2:1; 3:1). James revealed his loving heart toward his people, yet he remained strong in his exhortation.

   (2) "This you know"

   Some Bibles say "wherefore" at the beginning of verse 19. The Greek word translated "wherefore" is *hōste*. In the best Greek manuscripts the word is *histe*, which should be translated, "this you know." Such a translation fits much better with the use of *de* ("but") in verse 19, and makes sense in the context. So what did James mean? He was reacting to verse 18, saying in effect, "You know this. You know that the power of the Word was able to make you a new creation, the firstfruits of a glorious new creation that God will perform in the future."

   The people were aware of the marvelous power of the Word in regeneration. They knew that by His will He begot them with the Word of truth and made them new creations (James 1:18). They knew what it meant to be transformed by the incorruptible seed and given eternal life (1 Pet. 1:23).

Since they had experienced the power of the Word of God to make them new creations, they now had to allow it to continue to do its powerful work in their lives.

God brought us forth by the Word and wants us to live not by bread alone, but by every word that proceeds out of the mouth of God (Deut. 8:3). In fact, all Scripture is given "that the man of God may be perfect, thoroughly furnished unto all good works" (2 Tim. 3:17).

By continuing to hear the life-giving Word, your new nature is stimulated into action. Your spiritual dial is turned to God's channel, and you begin to receive His message. It all begins with an attitude of being receptive to God's Word. It is our food. In Jeremiah 15:16 the prophet says, "Thy words were found, and I did eat them."

b) A careful exposition (vv. 19*b*-20)

James says in verse 19, "Let every man be swift to hear, slow to speak, and slow to wrath."

(1) "Swift to hear"

(*a*) What it does not mean

Is James simply admonishing us to be good listeners and exercise caution when we speak? The book of Proverbs has much to say about the virtue of being such a person. "In the multitude of words there lacketh not sin, but he that refraineth his lips is wise" (Prov. 10:19). "He that keepeth his mouth keepeth his life, but he that openeth wide his lips shall have destruction" (Prov. 13:3). "Even a fool, when he holdeth his peace, is counted wise; and he that shutteth his lips is esteemed a man of understanding" (Prov. 17:28). "Seest thou a man that is hasty in his words? There is more hope of a fool than of him" (Prov. 29:20).

James, however, is not referring simply to the quality of our hearing or the economy of our words. The issue is far more profound.

(b) What it does mean

The issue is one's response to the Word. James referred to the Word of truth (v. 18), the engrafted Word (v. 21), and doers of the Word (v. 22). He called the Word a glass or mirror—the perfect law of liberty into which we look (vv. 23, 25). The Word of God is the theme.

To "be quick to listen" (NIV*) means to respond to the Word of God—to pursue every privileged occasion to learn more about God and His divine will. True believers are marked by such a pursuit. When we are faced with difficult trials that demand wisdom and strength from God, the Word provides the answers. When we face temptations that test us to the limit, the Word of God supplies the power to resist them. That's why the psalmist said, "Thy word have I hidden in mine heart, that I might not sin against thee" (Ps. 119:11).

The Word of God is our most welcome friend because it not only delivers us from trials and temptations but also engages us in communion with the living God. Such communion is the desire of every true believer.

Do You Have a Desire to Learn?

The psalmist said, "Thy testimonies have I taken as an heritage forever; for they are the rejoicing of my heart" (Ps. 119:111). Do you have such a hunger for God's Word? Charles Wesley wrote this short hymn on Deuteronomy 6:7 (*The Poetical Works of John and Charles Wesley*, vol. 9 [London: Wesleyan-Methodist, 1870], p. 94):

New International Version.

16

When quiet in my house I sit,
Thy book be my companion still,
My joy Thy sayings to repeat,
Talk o'er the records of Thy will,
And search the oracles Divine
Till every heartfelt word is mine.

Commentator J. A. Motyer said, "We might wonder why the ever-practical James does not proceed to outline schemes of daily Bible reading or the like, for surely these are the ways in which we offer a willing ear to the voice of God. But he does not help us in this way. Rather, he goes deeper, for there is little point in schemes and times if we have not got an attentive spirit. It is possible to be unfailingly regular in Bible reading, but achieve no more than to have moved the book-mark forward: this is reading unrelated to an attentive spirit. The Word is read but not heard. On the other hand, if we can develop an attentive spirit, this will spur us to create those conditions—a proper method in Bible reading, a discipline of time, and so on—by which the spirit will find itself satisfied in hearing the Word of God" (*The Message of James* [Downers Grove, Ill.: InterVarsity, 1985], pp. 64-65).

The true believer will have a desire for the Word of God. His desire may be dulled at times by the distractions of this world, but deep inside there remains a longing for the Word. Failure to satisfy such a longing results in greater spiritual hunger.

(2) "Slow to speak"

    (*a*) Defined

        i) What it does not mean

        James is not talking about our vocabulary, opinions, or social relationships.

        ii) What it does mean

        As quick as you are to listen, be that slow to speak. We are to pursue every opportunity to hear the Word of God, but exercise caution in assuming the role of a speaker.

(b) Demonstrated

i) James 3:1-2—"My brethren, be not many teachers, knowing that we shall receive the greater judgment. For in many things we all stumble. If any man offend not in word, the same is a perfect man, and able also to bridle the whole body." We all stumble and offend with our words. That's why we're not to rush into the role of a teacher.

ii) 1 Timothy 3:6—Paul gave this prohibition regarding church leaders: "Not a novice, lest being lifted up with pride he fall into the condemnation of the devil." No one should be placed into a leadership role if he is a novice in the faith. Violation of this principle could result in sinful pride.

iii) 1 Timothy 5:22—"Lay hands suddenly on no man." Leaders are not to be ordained too quickly.

iv) Ezekiel 3:17; 33:6-7—"Son of man, I have made thee a watchman unto the house of Israel; therefore, hear the word at my mouth, and give them warning from me. . . . But if the watchman see the sword come, and blow not the trumpet, and the people be not warned; if the sword come, and take any person from among them, he is taken away in his iniquity, but his blood will I require at the watchman's hand. So thou, O son of man, I have set thee a watchman unto the house of Israel; therefore, thou shalt hear the word at my mouth, and warn them from me." The ministry is a serious matter.

v) Hebrews 13:17—"Obey them that have the rule over you, and submit yourselves; for they watch for your souls, as they that must give account." Those in spiritual leadership are accountable to God for the faithfulness of their ministry. Therefore, believers should be quick to hear the Word they preach, yet reluctant to offer themselves in the role of a teacher.

Corresponding to the positive command to receive the Word with submissiveness is the negative command to exercise reluctance in becoming a teacher.

A Reluctance to Speak

When John Knox was called to preach he "burst forth in most abundant tears, and withdrew himself to his chamber. His countenance and behavior, from that day till the day that he was compelled to present himself to the public place of preaching, did sufficiently declare the grief and trouble of his heart" (William Barclay, *The Letters to Timothy, Titus, and Philemon* [Philadelphia: Westminster, 1975], pp. 49-50). For John Knox, the call to speak for God was an awesome responsibility. His attitude is commendable. There must be a certain reluctance to speak if one is ever to have anything worthwhile to say.

(c) Described

The extent of the problem of uncontrolled speech within the fellowship is evident by the number of verses James devotes to the issue.

i) James 1:26—"If any man among you seem to be religious, and bridleth not his tongue, but deceiveth his own heart, this man's religion is vain." Many would-be teachers were deceivers, and their religion was useless.

ii) James 3:1—"My brethren, be not many teachers, knowing that we shall receive the greater judgment." James goes on for the following seventeen verses to talk

19

about the tongue and the importance of keeping it under control.

iii) James 4:6-12—"God resisteth the proud, but giveth grace unto the humble. Submit yourselves, therefore, to God. Resist the devil, and he will flee from you. Draw near to God, and he will draw near to you. Cleanse your hands, ye sinners; and purify your hearts, ye double-minded. Be afflicted, and mourn, and weep; let your laughter be turned to mourning, and your joy to heaviness. Humble yourselves in the sight of the Lord, and he shall lift you up. Speak not evil one of another, brethren. He that speaketh evil of his brother, and judgeth his brother, speaketh evil of the law, and judgeth the law; but if thou judge the law, thou are not a doer of the law but a judge. There is one lawgiver, who is able to save and to destroy. Who art thou that judgest another?" Perhaps there were proud people in the assembly who wanted to be heard. James instructed them to be humble and stop speaking evil of one another.

iv) James 5:9—"Murmur not one against another, brethren, lest ye be judged; behold, the judge standeth before the door."

Believers are to take every opportunity to listen to the Word, but are to be slow in becoming teachers. Believers who do teach must have a thoroughly prepared heart and speak God's truth accurately.

(3) "Slow to wrath"

(a) Defined

James is not speaking of outward bursts of anger (Gk., *thumos*) but of a deep internal resentment accompanied by an attitude of

20

rejection (Gk., *orgē*). If the Word of God disagrees with our opinions or confronts our sin, we must submit to it rather than resent it. Those who confront us with the Word are to be received rather than rejected.

(*b*) Demonstrated

  i) James 4:1-3—"From where come wars and fightings among you? Come they not here, even of your lusts that war in your members? Ye lust, and have not; ye kill, and desire to have, and cannot obtain; ye fight and war, yet ye have not, because ye ask not. Ye ask, and receive not, because ye ask amiss, that ye may consume it upon your lusts." Why was there such anger and hostility? Because they were pitted against each other. Everyone had an opinion and wanted to be heard.

  ii) Galatians 4:16—Paul said, "Am I, therefore, become your enemy, because I tell you the truth?" Some of the Galatians resented Paul's teaching because it exposed their sin.

(*c*) Defended

James 1:20 says, "The wrath of man worketh not the righteousness of God." An attitude of resentment and rejection toward the Word of God cannot produce a life-style that is pleasing to God.

There is righteous anger, as demonstrated by Jesus when He "found in the temple those that sold oxen and sheep and doves, and the changers of money, sitting. And when he had made a scourge of small cords, he drove them all out of the temple. . . . And said unto them that sold doves, Take these things from here; make not my Father's house an house of merchandise" (John 2:14-16). However, James is not referring to that kind of anger, but to sinful anger.

Believers are to take every opportunity to listen to the Word of God, exercise a reluctance to speak until they are thoroughly prepared, patiently accept what is taught, and guard against an attitude of resentment.

B. A Willingness to Receive the Word with Purity (v. 21a)

"Wherefore, put away all filthiness and overflowing of wickedness."

1. The principle

We must receive the Word with a pure life. Anger and other sins are displeasing to God and will hinder the production of His righteousness in our lives.

2. The particulars

a) The action

James instructs us to "put away . . . and receive." The key word is "receive," but there is a vital word before receive—the Greek participle *apotithēminoi*, which means "having put off." The aorist tense of both the main verb ("receive") and the participle ("having put off") emphasizes the importance of putting off sin prior to receiving the Word.

According to Greek scholars Fritz Rienecker and Cleon Rogers, the verb *apotithēmi* originally meant to put off one's clothes—to take off dirty, soiled clothes (*Linguistic Key to the Greek New Testament* [Grand Rapids: Zondervan, 1980], p. 725). The verb form is used elsewhere in the New Testament to illustrate the necessity of putting aside sin before spiritual growth can occur.

(1) Ephesians 4:22—"Put off concerning the former manner of life the old man, which is corrupt according to the deceitful lusts."

(2) Colossians 3:8—"Ye also put off all these: anger, wrath, malice, blasphemy, filthy communication out of your mouth."

(3) Hebrews 12:1—"Let us lay aside every weight, and the sin which doth so easily beset us."

(4) 1 Peter 2:1-2—"Laying aside all malice, and all guile, and hypocrisies, and envies, and all evil speakings, as newborn babes, desire the pure milk of the word, that ye may grow by it."

b) The evil

"Filthiness" (Gk., *rhuparia*) is used of dirty clothes as well as of moral vice. The root word is *rhupos*, which was sometimes used to refer to wax in the ear. Just as wax in the ear impedes our natural hearing, sin in our lives impedes reception of God's Word.

"Wickedness" (Gk., *kakia*) refers to any evil intent or desire. James may be saying to put aside all evil actions (filthiness) as well as evil intentions (wickedness). "Overflowing" (Gk., *perisseia*) refers to an abundance. All abundant, prevailing evil must be put aside through confession and repentance.

3. The pattern

In 1 Thessalonians 2:13-14 Paul says, "When ye received the word of God which ye heard of us, ye received it, not as the word of men but as it is in truth, the word of God, which effectually worketh also in you that believe. For ye, brethren, became followers of the churches of God which in Judaea are in Christ Jesus." The Thessalonian believers heard the Word of God with unstopped ears.

C. A Willingness to Receive the Word with Humility (v. 21*b*)

"Receive with meekness the engrafted word, which is able to save your souls."

1. How do we receive it?

   "Meekness" (Gk., *prautēs*) could be translated "humble," "gentle," "meek," or "a willing spirit"; but the best translation is "teachable." A submissive, pure, humble heart is a teachable heart. "Receive" is an urgent command.

   We are to receive the Word with a teachable spirit—without resentment, anger, or pride.

2. What do we receive?

   James describes the Word as that which is engrafted or implanted (Gk., *emphutos*). The Word of God, implanted by the Holy Spirit within the heart of the believer at the time of salvation, is the vital element of our new life. James says the power and effect of that rooted Word is dependent on our willingness to receive it.

3. Why do we receive it?

   James uses a present participle to describe the work of the Word within the believer: It is able to continually save his soul.

   a) Romans 13:11—"Now is our salvation nearer than when we believed." Scripture teaches a past, present, and future aspect to our salvation. We are saved, but the fullness of our salvation is not yet realized—we are not yet glorified. The Word of God sustains and nurtures us throughout that process.

   b) Romans 1:16—"I am not ashamed of the gospel of Christ; for it is the power of God unto salvation to everyone that believeth."

   c) Hebrews 4:12—"The word of God is living, and powerful, and sharper than any two-edged sword, piercing even to the dividing asunder of soul and spirit, and of the joints and marrow, and is a discerner of the thoughts and intents of the heart."

By the power of the Word the believer has been saved from the penalty of sin, is being saved from the power of sin, and will ultimately be saved from the presence of sin.

Conclusion

James is calling us to a right reception of the Word of God. How are we to listen? With a submissive, pure, and humble heart. Such is the mark of a true believer.

Focusing on the Facts

1. What is the attitude of a believer toward the Word of God (see p. 9)?
2. What is the attitude of an unbeliever toward the Word of God (see p. 9)?
3. According to Psalm 119:155, what is the consequence of avoiding God's Word (see p. 9)?
4. What should be the prayer of the believer at times of temptation (Psalm 119:36-37; see p. 10)?
5. What three tests for true faith are given by James (see p. 11)?
6. What does it mean to "receive" the Word (v. 19; see pp. 12-13)?
7. What is the role of God's Word in nurturing the believer's new life (see p. 15)?
8. Explain what James means by being "quick to listen" (v. 19; see p. 16).
9. Review the section entitled "Do You Have a Desire to Listen?" (see pp. 16-17). Is there any difference between reading the Bible and being quick to listen? Explain (see p. 17).
10. What does the reaction of John Knox to his call to preach the Word illustrate about the importance of being "slow to speak" (v. 19; see p. 19)?
11. What type of anger was James referring to when he said "be slow to wrath" (v. 19; see pp. 20-21)?
12. In what ways did the audience to whom James wrote show its resentment of Scripture (James 4:1-3; see p. 21)?
13. What is the significance of the Greek participle translated "put away" (v. 21; see p. 22)?

14. Is there a difference between "filthiness" and "wickedness" (v. 21)? If so, what is it (see p. 23)?
15. What is an attitude of meekness, and how does it relate to our ability to properly receive the Word of God (see p. 24)?

Pondering the Principles

1. The psalmist wrote, "I have inclined mine heart to perform thy statutes always, even unto the end" (Ps. 119:112). His prayer reflects a lifelong commitment to obey the Word of God. Does his prayer reflect the commitment of your heart? Or have you allowed yourself to be distracted from the blessing and strength that come from sweet communion with God through His Word? If so, ask God's forgiveness, and reaffirm your desire to be one of whom it is said, "His delight is in the law of the Lord; and in [God's] law doth he meditate day and night" (Ps. 1:2).

2. We've seen that there is a significant difference between *reading* the Word and *responding* to the Word (see p. 17). Ask God to create within you an attentive spirit. Cultivate the discipline of spending time in the Word daily with the goal of responding. Find a family member or friend with whom you can establish accountability and tell him or her what you are discovering from the Word.

3. How do you respond when the Word of God exposes sin in your life? Do you accept or reject its message? How do you feel about those who confront you with the Word? Is there a sense of humble submission, or do you harbor resentment toward them? Remember, it is not enough to say you believe the gospel or trust in God's Word. The test of true faith is your response to the authority of the Word.

2
The Belief That Behaves—Part 2

Outline

Introduction
A. Conduct: The Test of a Person's Character
  1. Stated
  2. Supported
    a) Matthew 7:17-18
    b) Proverbs 4:23
    c) Matthew 12:34-35
B. Obedience: The Test of a Person's Faith
  1. The friends of Christ
    a) John 15:14
    b) John 14:23
    c) 1 John 2:3
  2. The enemies of Christ
    a) John 14:24
    b) 1 John 2:4

Review
I. A Proper Reception of the Word (vv. 19-21)
  A. A Willingness to Receive the Word with Submission (vv. 19-20)
  B. A Willingness to Receive the Word with Purity (v. 21*a*)
  C. A Willingness to Receive the Word with Humility (v. 21*b*)

Lesson
II. A Proper Reaction to the Word (vv. 22-27)
  A. A Willingness to Apply the Word Without Deception (vv. 22*b*-26)
    1. The deception of hearing without responding (vv. 22*b*-25)

a) The deception defined (v. 22*b*)
b) The deception illustrated (vv. 23-24)
    (1) The subject (v. 23*a*)
    (2) The action (v. 23*b*)
    (3) The object (v. 23*c*)
    (4) The results (v. 24)
c) The deception contrasted (v. 25)
    (1) The subject (v. 25*d-e*)
    (2) The action (v. 25*b*)
    (3) The object (v. 25*c*)
    (4) The results (v. 25*d-f*)
        (*a*) He is a persevering learner (v. 25*d*)
        (*b*) He is a doer of the work (v. 25*e*)
        (*c*) He is blessed in his deed (v. 25*f*)

Conclusion

Introduction

A. Conduct: The Test of a Person's Character

1. Stated

   The character of a person, whether godly or evil, is demonstrated by his conduct.

2. Supported

   a) Matthew 7:17-18—With great certainty Jesus said, "Every good tree bringeth forth good fruit, but a corrupt tree bringeth forth bad fruit. A good tree cannot bring forth bad fruit, neither can a corrupt tree bring forth good fruit."

   b) Proverbs 4:23—"Keep thy heart with all diligence; for out of it are the issues of life." A good heart produces good; an evil heart produces evil.

   c) Matthew 12:34-35—"Out of the abundance of the heart the mouth speaketh. A good man out of the good treasure of the heart bringeth forth good things, and an evil man out of the evil treasure bringeth forth evil things."

B. Obedience: The Test of a Person's Faith

1. The friends of Christ

Godly conduct is a test of genuine love for Christ.

a) John 15:14—Jesus said, "Ye are my friends, if ye do whatever I command you."

b) John 14:23—Jesus also said, "If a man love me, he will keep my words."

c) 1 John 2:3—The apostle John wrote, "By this we do know that we know him, if we keep his commandments."

2. The enemies of Christ

Hostility toward Christ is also demonstrated in conduct.

a) John 14:24—"He that loveth me not keepeth not my sayings."

b) 1 John 2:4—"He that saith, I know him, and keepeth not his commandments, is a liar, and the truth is not in him."

Obedience is the dividing line between saint and sinner. First John 3:10 says, "In this the children of God are manifest, and the children of the devil: whosoever doeth not righteousness is not of God, neither he that loveth not his brother." It's not a question of what we claim but of how we live. Obedience to the Word of God is the most basic spiritual requirement and the common denominator of all true believers. Those who disobey the Word of God reveal an absence of the life of God in their souls.

James 1:22 says, "Be ye doers of the word and not hearers only, deceiving your own selves." If you are a hearer only, you are deceiving yourself about your salvation, your genuineness, your authenticity as a Christian. A desire to obey the Word of God—to be a doer, not merely a hearer—is a mark of true saving faith.

Review

James gives three tests of true faith. The first two tests involve our response to trials and temptations. The third test, our response to the Word of God, is perhaps the most salient test of all. Are you content simply to hear the Word being taught, or do you have a deep desire to obey it? Such a desire is a sure indicator of the life of God within you.

Key Elements of Spiritual Revival

The book of Nehemiah illustrates a proper response to the Word of God. In 605 B.C. Jerusalem was destroyed by Nebuchadnezzar, and the Jews were taken captive to Babylon. After seventy years of captivity some of the Jewish people returned to Jerusalem (Ezra 1-2). Their first order of business was to rebuild the Temple, which was accomplished under the leadership of Zerubbabel (Ezra 3-6).

The Jewish people's next task was to rebuild the city walls so that Jerusalem would once again be safe from attack. They did so in only fifty-two days by the power of the Spirit and under the leadership of Nehemiah, a fellow Jewish captive to Babylon who had served as cup bearer to King Artaxerxes I (Neh. 1:1–7:4).

As the Jewish people witnessed the faithfulness of God in restoring them to the land and rebuilding their Temple and city walls, the stage was set for a spiritual revival. The key elements of that revival are recorded in the book of Nehemiah.

1. The presentation of God's Word

    Nehemiah 8:1 says, "All the people gathered themselves together as one man into the street that was before the water gate; and they spoke unto Ezra, the scribe, to bring the book of the law of Moses, which the Lord had commanded to Israel." Revival always begins with the Word of God.

Verses 2-3, 5 tell us that "Ezra, the priest, brought the law before the congregation both of men and women, and all who could hear with understanding, upon the first day of the seventh month. And he read from it facing the street that was before the water gate from the morning until midday, before the men and the women, and those who could understand; and the ears of all the people were attentive unto the book of the law. . . . And Ezra opened the book in the sight of all the people (for he was above all the people); and when he opened it, all the people stood up." They not only listened all day, but also listened standing up.

Then "Ezra blessed the Lord, the great God. And all the people answered, Amen, Amen, lifting up their hands; and they bowed their heads, and worshiped the Lord with their faces to the ground" (v. 6). The people were humbled as they heard the Word of God.

2. The explanation of God's Word

Ezra had people assisting him who "caused the people to understand the law. . . . So they read in the book in the law of God distinctly, and gave the sense, and caused them to understand the reading" (vv. 7-8). It is not enough to read the Word; there must also be an explanation of its meaning.

3. The response to God's Word

a) Their confession

Nehemiah said, "This day is holy unto the Lord, your God; mourn not, nor weep. For all the people wept, when they heard the words of the law" (v. 9). When the people heard the Word of God, it convicted them of their sin, and they began to mourn and weep.

The first three verses of chapter 9 say, "Now in the twenty and fourth day of this month the children of Israel were assembled with fasting, in sackcloth, and with earth upon them. And the seed of Israel separated themselves from all foreigners, and stood and confessed their sins and the iniquities of their fathers. And they stood up in their place, and read in the book of the law of the Lord, their God, one fourth part of the day; and another fourth part they confessed, and worshiped the Lord, their God." Confession of sin is part of revival. The preaching and exposition of the Word penetrates the heart and elicits confession of sin.

b) Their celebration

Nehemiah replied, "Go your way, eat the fat, and drink the sweet, and send portions unto them for whom nothing is prepared; for this day is holy unto our Lord. Neither be ye grieved; for the joy of the Lord is your strength. So the Levites stilled all the people, saying, Hold your peace; for the day is holy, neither be ye grieved. And all the people went their way to eat, and to drink, and to send portions, and to make great mirth, because they had understood the words that were declared unto them" (8:10-12). Not only was there a message in the Word of God about sin, but there was also a message about forgiveness. Therefore the people experienced mixed emotions: sorrow over sin and celebration because of forgiveness.

c) Their covenant

(1) Nehemiah 9:38—"Because of all this we make a sure covenant, and write it; and our princes, Levites, and priests, set their seal to it." The first twenty-eight verses of chapter 10 lists the names of everyone who affirmed the covenant.

(2) Nehemiah 10:28-29—"The rest of the people, the priests, the Levites, the porters, the singers, the Nethinims, and all they who had separated themselves from the people of the lands unto the law of God, their wives, their sons, and their daughters, everyone having knowledge, and having understanding; they did cleave to their brethren, their nobles, and entered into a curse, and into an oath, to walk in God's law, which was given by Moses, the servant of God, and to observe and do all the commandments of the Lord, our Lord, and his ordinances and his statutes." The Word of God elicited a covenant of obedience. The people made a vow that involved a curse should they disobey.

(3) Luke 6:46-49—Jesus said, "Why call ye me, Lord, Lord, and do not the things which I say? Whosoever cometh to me, and heareth my sayings, and doeth them, I will show you to whom he is like: he is like a man who built an house, and dug deep, and laid the foundation on a rock; and when a flood arose, the stream beat vehemently upon that house, and could not shake it; for it was founded upon a rock. But he that heareth, and doeth not, is like a man that, without a foundation, built an house upon the earth, against which the stream did beat vehemently, and immediately it fell; and the ruin of that house was great." If we attempt to construct a religious house on anything other than obedience to the Word of God, our effort is folly.

I remember hearing many formulas about the Christian life when I was growing up, and I admit that I tried many of them. For example, someone would give me a book and say, "This will tell you how to be totally committed to God." I would read all the formulas, pray the prayer, and not see any major change in my life. It took me a long time to realize that the bottom line in one's spiritual life is not a momentary commitment but a long-term pattern of obedience. There must be a point in time when you covenant to be obedient to the Word of God. As you do your best in the energy of the Spirit to live out that covenant, you manifest a genuine salvation. Even if you sense conviction of sin and a desire for the forgiveness God provides, if you don't long to obey God, what you think is saving faith is something less, and you are deceived.

(4) James 1:18-19—"Of his own will begot he us with the word of truth, that we should be a kind of first fruits of his creatures. Wherefore, my beloved brethren, let every man be swift to hear, slow to speak, slow to wrath." We were begotten with the Word of truth. The Word of God than becomes the focal point of that new life as we continue to be obedient to it. How we respond to the Word of God is indicative of our spiritual state.

James makes two points regarding a proper response to God's Word.

I. A PROPER RECEPTION OF THE WORD (vv. 19-21; see pp. 12-25)

  A. A Willingness to Receive the Word with Submission (vv. 19-20; see pp. 13-22)

  B. A Willingness to Receive the Word with Purity (v. 21a; see pp. 22-23)

  C. A Willingness to Receive the Word with Humility (v. 21b; see pp. 23-25)

Lesson

II. A PROPER REACTION TO THE WORD (vv. 22-27)

Doers of the Word

James exhorted his readers, saying, "Be ye doers of the word and not hearers only, deceiving your own selves" (v. 22).

1. The conjunction

The word *but* is extremely important here. It is wonderful to hear the Word with submission, purity, and humility, but hearing isn't enough. We must go one step further—we must become doers. The Word of God must be obeyed in daily life.

2. The command

The present imperative sense of the verb indicates that we're to keep on striving to be doers of the Word.

Commentator D. Edmond Hiebert said, "This would be nothing new to the Jewish readers of James, since 'doing the Word' was a familiar maxim in Jewish ethical literature" (*The Epistle of James* [Chicago: Moody, 1979], p. 132). The rabbis taught that one ought not only read the laws of Moses but also practice what they command (cf. Babylonian Talmud *Aboth* 11).

So do true believers put the Word into practice? Yes. Do they *always* put the Word into practice? No—or a pastor's task would be relatively simple. But even when Christians fail to apply the Word, they recognize their failure and desire greater consistency in being doers of the Word.

Many of the Jewish people of Jesus' day attended the reading and exposition of the Word, yet did absolutely nothing about it. But James says that hearing is not enough. We must apply what we hear and become doers of the Word.

3. The contrast

   a) "Doers"

   Why did James use a substantive (a word or phrase used as a noun—"be ye doers") instead of saying "do the word"? Perhaps because the word *doer* carries with it a characterization of a whole personality. It's one thing to fight in a war; it's something else to be a soldier. It's one thing to build a house; it's something else to be a builder. It's one thing to teach someone; it's something else to be a teacher. To be a soldier, builder, or teacher is characteristic of one's life. Characteristically we are to be doers of the Word.

   James used the Greek word translated "doer" three times in this portion of Scripture and once in chapter 4 ("a doer of the law," v. 11). Commentator Robert Johnstone described the doer as one possessing "a life of holy energy" (*Lectures Exegetical and Practical on the Epistle of James* [Minneapolis: Klock & Klock, 1978], p. 143).

   b) "Hearers"

   Hearing is important (vv. 19-21), but we are not to be "hearers only" (v. 22). The Greek verb translated "hearer" (*akroatēs*) is the ancient term for auditors. Have you ever gone to school and audited a class? When you audit a class you listen to the lectures but don't do the required assignments. We have a lot of spiritual auditors in the church. "I want to come to church, but I don't want to get involved." They come in, listen to the sermon, and leave. There is no change in their lives. They have the privilege of hearing the Word, but they have no commitment to doing the work of the ministry.

Hearing the Word of God is not an end in itself—it's a means to an end. The end is obedience. If you come to church and hear the Word being taught yet nothing changes in your life, you may think yourself to be religious and to trust in God and to have saving faith, but you are deceived.

The test of saving faith is a willingness to receive the Word and respond to it in daily life.

Just as there are three elements involved in receiving the Word—submission, purity, and humility—there are also three elements involved in responding to the Word.

A. A Willingness to Apply the Word Without Deception (vv. 22b-26)

1. The deception of hearing without responding (vv. 22b-25)

a) The deception defined (v. 22b)

"Deceiving your own selves."

If you are hearers only, you are self-deceived. It's like the old Scottish phrase that speaks of "sermon tasters who never tasted the grace of God." Any response to the Word of truth other than obedience is merely a deception. Sentimental admiration of the preacher, intellectual stimulation, or the emotional exhilaration of discovering truth are all merely deceptions if nothing happens in your life. Satan would love to make you content with that level of religious involvement.

The Greek word translated "deceiving" in verse 22 (*paralogizomai*) means "to reason beside, or alongside." We might say it means to be beside yourself. When that word appears in secular mathematical terminology it means to miscalculate—to reckon wrongly. If you think that hearing the Word of God is enough, you have made a gross miscalculation. You are self-deceived through fallacious reasoning. You are beside yourself. You have misconstrued true godliness. In addition to hearing the Word you must apply it.

Robert Johnstone said, "Knowing that the study of divine truth, through reading the Bible, giving attendance on the public ordinances of grace, and otherwise, is a most important duty,—is, indeed, the road leading toward the gate of everlasting life,—they allow themselves, through man's natural aversion to all genuine spirituality, to be persuaded by the wicked one that this is the sum of all Christian duty, and itself the gate of life, so that in mere 'hearing' they enter in, and all is well with them. To rest satisfied with the means of grace, without yielding up our hearts to their power as means, so as to receive the grace and exhibit its working in our lives, is manifestly folly of the same class as that of a workman who should content himself with possessing tools, without using them,—madness of the same class as that of a man perishing with hunger, who should exult in having bread in his hands, without eating it,—but folly and madness as immeasurably greater than these, as the 'work of God' (John vi.29) transcends in importance the work of an earthly artisan, and 'life with Christ in God' the perishable existence of earth" (p. 144).

We would say a person was foolish to die of hunger with bread in his hands. Just as foolish is one who hears and does not do.

b) The deception illustrated (vv. 23-24)

To explain this deception, James presents a vivid word picture.

(1) The subject (v. 23*a*)

"If anyone be a hearer of the word, and not a doer."

If anyone is a "hearer of the word, and not a doer," he has taken the deceitful route. James goes on to give a graphic illustration of someone who hears but does not respond.

(2) The action (v. 23b)

"He is like a man beholding."

Contrary to some commentators, "beholding" does not mean "to take a casual glance." The word translated "beholding" (Gk., *katanoeō*) is a forceful word. It means to look carefully, cautiously, observantly.

(3) The object (v. 23c)

"His natural face in a mirror."

"His natural face" is literally translated "the face of his birth." He looks into a mirror and sees his face. Glass mirrors weren't as common as metallic mirrors during the Roman Empire. The metallic mirrors were made of bronze, silver, or—for the wealthy—gold. The metal was beaten flat, then polished to a high gloss. The image reflected by such mirrors was adequate, though not perfect. That's why Paul said, "Now we see in a mirror, darkly [indistinctly]; but then, face to face" (1 Cor. 13:12).

(4) The results (v. 24)

"He beholdeth himself, and goeth his way, and immediately forgetteth what manner of man he was."

He looks at himself and then leaves. With a mirror no longer in front of him, he immediately forgets what he looks like.

Have you ever had that happen to you? At times I have been sitting at my desk and touched my face, only to realize that I had missed a spot when shaving. I had been been interrupted by a phone call or by my wife's call to breakfast. Women, perhaps you have been distracted by your children to the point of forgetting a portion of your make-up, yet you don't discover the oversight until later. Those are examples of looking into a mirror and then immediately forgetting what we saw.

The point is this: If you don't do something on the spot when you see what needs to be done, you'll get busy in life and forget that anything needs to be done at all. You've got to do it while you're aware of it. For example, by Monday morning most people have forgotten Sunday's sermon. If you don't make the necessary corrections when God is impressing them upon your heart, you may never get around to it. You might forget. The image reflected in the mirror of God's Word will soon fade.

c) The deception contrasted (v. 25)

"Whosoever looketh into the perfect law of liberty, and continueth in it, he being not a forgetful hearer but a doer of the work, this man shall be blessed in his deed."

(1) The subject (v. 25d-e)

"But whosoever . . . being not a forgetful hearer but a doer of the work."

Verse 25 clarifies the analogy by contrasting the forgetful hearer with the one in whom the Word produces a response.

(2) The action (v. 25b)

"Looketh."

The word translated "looketh" (Gk., parakuptō) is not the same word used in verse 23 for "beholding" (Gk., katanoeō). Parakuptō literally means "to stoop over" or "to bend down to examine something with care and precision." The stooping im-

39

plies a humbling of oneself—looking intently with great desire and effort at the mirror, wanting to discern what is revealed.

Are You Prepared to Receive Scripture?

Your attitude in approaching the Word of God is vital. Do you prepare your heart before you read, study, or hear the Lord's Word proclaimed by saying, "God, I want to look into the mirror and see exactly what my natural face looks like. I want to see all the blemishes and blotches and all the places that need repair. Lord, I come with a heart that desires You to show me where the problem areas are in my life so I can see them changed." Is that your attitude?

(3) The object (v. 25c)

"Into the perfect law of liberty."

To understand what the perfect law of liberty is, we must realize that the only perfect law ever given was God's law. Scripture tells us how to be free from the bondage of sin—it is the source of all of our liberty. We need to gaze upon the only authoritative instruction from God.

The Perfect Law of Liberty

God's Word is called "the law" in both the Old and New Testaments. It is the law of the Lord—an obligatory behavioral code. The presence of God's grace does not imply the absence of God's law. Because there is forgiveness when we break it does not mean there is no law. There is a moral law that God wants us to obey. Jesus came to fulfill that law, not to set it aside (Matt. 5:17-20).

God's law is perfect. It's complete. It's sufficient. It's comprehensive. It represents the revelation of God's will for mankind. It is completely without error. It can meet every need, touch every part of life, fulfill every desire of every heart. It is the law of God. As we look into that law, it liberates us. Yet what a paradox! So often we think of law and freedom as opposites. But as the Spirit of God enables us to apply the principles of God's Word, we are freed from bondage to sin and enabled to honor God through righteous living. That is true freedom!

(4) The results (v. 25*d-f*)

(*a*) He is a persevering learner (v. 25*d*)

"And continueth in it."

James distinguishes the hearer from the one who looks into the Word of God and continues in it. The implication is that he keeps on looking. He is a persevering learner.

Are You a Persevering Learner?

A persevering learner is one who carefully considers whatever the Word of God reveals about himself. He sees all that is wrong in his life and unpleasing to God, and wants to get rid of it. That's the kind of character that marks a true believer.

I believe that man's natural aversion to serious spiritual thought is a serious obstacle to salvation. People don't want to do a serious self-examination. But he who knows the Lord must long to see himself as he is. Do you want to become more like Christ? Do you want to deal with whatever blemishes the Word of God reveals in your life? Do you come before God and say, "Show me where my failures are; show me the ugliness of my sin so I can come to You for the cure"?

A persevering learner stoops down to examine the Word of God carefully. He sees it as a liberating law, not a law of bondage. He continues to examine it and is not a forgetful hearer. Perhaps he goes home from church and reads the passage that's been taught before he goes to sleep. Perhaps he reviews the passage every day for the next week and cries out, "God, change my life!"

Can you imagine what would happen if people began to live like that? So often we think we've done our spiritual duty when we've listened. But that's just the beginning! Do you continue to look into the Word of God until it tells you who you are and where you're at so that you call on God to make the necessary changes?

41

(*b*) He is a doer of the work (v. 25*e*)

"He being not a forgetful hearer but a doer of the work."

A doer of the Word (v. 23) is a doer of God's work (v. 25). The Christian sees things as they really are, and his will is brought into union with God's will. He loves to do what the Bible commands to be done.

(*c*) He is blessed in his deed (v. 25*f*)

"This man shall be blessed in his deed."

The blessing is not in the hearing, but in the doing. Joshua 1:8 says, "This book of the law shall not depart out of thy mouth, but thou shall meditate therein day and night, that thou mayest observe to do according to all that is written therein; for then thou shalt make thy way prosperous, and then thou shalt have good success." If you want to be successful, obey the Word—look into it, meditate on it day and night, and allow it to change your life as it reveals who you are.

The wonderful truth is that he who looks into the perfect law of liberty and continues in it finds it to be a yoke that is "easy" and a burden that is "light" (Matt. 11:30)—just as Jesus promised.

Conclusion

The hearer and the doer are similar in several ways. They look at the law of God, they listen, to some degree they are intent in their observation, and they are seeing the problems in their lives. The difference is that one immediately makes a covenant with God to be obedient, whereas the other does not. In fact, the forgetful hearer may feel resentment toward the Word for having exposed his sin.

Many years ago I invited a Scottish evangelist to speak to a college group. As he spoke, some of the things he said touched my heart. Afterwards I went up to him and with sincerity said, "I want you to know that what you said ministered to me, and I'm very appreciative." I'll never forget his abrupt reply. He said, "Well, what are you going to do about it?" and walked away. I admit that for many years I did not like him. I thought to myself, *He certainly could have shown a little common courtesy. I was just trying to be nice!* But his reply stuck in my mind. I have forgotten many of the conversations I've had over the years, but I remember that one.

What are you going to do about what you learn from the Word of God? The doer puts the Word into practice by applying it to his daily living. The result is spiritual growth and progress. That is true faith at work. It's more than the momentary experience of hearing—it's a life-style of response to God's truth.

Focusing on the Facts

1. According to Matthew 12:33-35, how is a man's character demonstrated (see pp. 28-29)?
2. How does a person know if he has a saving knowledge of the Lord (John 14:23; 1 John 2:3; see p. 29)?
3. How did the apostle John label a person who claims to know Christ yet does not obey Him (1 John 2:4; see p. 29)?
4. What is the primary distinction between a saint and a sinner (1 John 3:10; see p. 29)?
5. What are the key elements of spiritual revival (see pp. 30-31)?
6. Review the three responses to the Word of God in Nehemiah 8-9 (see pp. 31-33). In your opinion, is any one of the responses more important than the others? Why?
7. Why do various formulas about the Christian life tend to fall short of providing true spiritual growth (see p. 33)?
8. What does it mean to be a doer of the Word (see p. 35)?
9. What does a hearer of the Word have in common with a student who audits a class (see pp. 35-36)?
10. The Greek word *paralogizomai*, translated "deceiving" in James 1:22, had an interesting meaning in secular Greek mathematics. What was that meaning, and how could it apply to one who hears the Word of God but doesn't apply what he hears (see pp. 36-37)?

11. How does James illustrate the spiritual attitude of one who simply hears the Word (vv. 23-24; see pp. 37-39)? What principle is James communicating through that illustration (see p. 39)?
12. How does the "looking" of James 1:25 differ from the "beholding" of James 1:23 (see pp. 39-40)?
13. What does James mean by "the perfect law of liberty" (v. 25; see pp. 40-41)?
14. Describe a persevering learner (see p. 41).
15. According to James 1:25, how does a man obtain the blessing of God (see p. 42)?

Pondering the Principles

1. Review the section entitled "Key Elements of Spiritual Revival" (see pp. 30-33). When asked about their relationship with the Lord, most Christians recount how and when they became a Christian. But a more probing question is: What evidence do you currently see in your life to indicate the presence of saving faith? Whenever true spiritual revival takes place, the result is a covenant of obedience to God. Is your life marked by a pattern of obedience? Such is the evidence of true faith. Daily seek the Lord's grace and wisdom to help you live in obedience to His Word.

2. Unfortunately, some Christians are so caught up in the pursuit of entertainment and other distractions that they have little time for serious self-examination. The apostle Paul exhorted us to examine ourselves to see if we are in the faith (2 Cor. 13:5) and instructed those at the Lord's Table to examine themselves carefully lest they incur the judgment of God for partaking in an unworthy manner (1 Cor. 11:28-30). According to James, the person who looks intently into the Word of God and continues in it is committed to serious self-examination. Are you? Make the commitment to face what needs changing in your life, and trust God for results.

3. Review the section entitled "Are You a Persevering Learner?" (see p. 41). Do you willingly submit your life to the probing light of God's Word, or do you tend to avoid it? Remember, God looks upon the heart—nothing is hidden from Him. Therefore

the issue in self-examination and confession of sin is not to inform God of something He doesn't know. The issue is your being honest with Him. Be a persevering learner. Continually expose your heart and mind to God's truth, with the prayer that He will change whatever needs to be changed. Echo the words of the psalmist who said, "Search me, O God, and know my heart; try me, and know my thoughts; and see if there be any wicked way in me, and lead me in the way everlasting" (Ps. 139:23-24).

3
The Belief That Behaves—Part 3

Outline

Introduction
A. The Passage
B. The Problem
   1. Stated
   2. Illustrated
      a) Matthew 25:1-13
      b) 1 John
      c) James

Review
 I. A Proper Reception of the Word (vv. 19-21)
    A. A Willingness to Receive the Word with Submission (vv. 19-20)
    B. A Willingness to Receive the Word with Purity (v. 21*a*)
    C. A Willingness to Receive the Word with Humility (v. 21*b*)
II. A Proper Reaction to the Word (vv. 22-27)
    A. A Willingness to Apply the Word Without Deception (vv. 22-26)
       1. The deception of hearing without responding (vv. 22*b*-25)

Lesson
    2. The deception of responding without exercising self-control (v. 26)
       a) A wrong opinion
       b) An uncontrolled tongue
       c) An external formality
       d) An unholy heart
       e) A useless religion

B. A Willingness to Apply the Word Without Selfishness (v. 27a)
1. The nature of true religion
2. The judge of true religion
3. The activity of true religion
   a) Explained
   b) Exemplified
      (1) Matthew 25:35-36
      (2) 1 John 2:10-11
      (3) 1 John 3:10-18
4. The recipients of true religion
   a) Explained
   b) Exemplified
C. A Willingness to Apply the Word Without Compromise (v. 27b)
1. The exhortation
2. The example
Conclusion

Introduction

A. The Passage

James 1:22-27 says, "Be ye doers of the word and not hearers only, deceiving your own selves. For if any be a hearer of the word, and not a doer, he is like a man beholding his natural face in a mirror; for he beholdeth himself, and goeth his way, and immediately forgetteth what manner of man he was. But whosoever looketh into the perfect law of liberty, and continueth in it, he being not a forgetful hearer but a doer of the work, this man shall be blessed in his deed. If any man among you seem to be religious, and bridleth not his tongue, but deceiveth his own heart, this man's religion is vain. Pure religion and undefiled before God and the Father is this: to visit the fatherless and widows in their affliction, and to keep oneself unspotted from the world."

B. The Problem

1. Stated

Scripture repeatedly speaks of those who have a form of godliness but deny the power thereof (2 Tim. 3:5). Not only are there saved people and lost people, but there are also lost people who believe they are saved. Such deception is of tremendous concern to God because it is eternally fatal. Therefore, the cry of the Spirit of God throughout the Old and New Testaments is that a person should not be deceived about the reality of his faith.

2. Illustrated

a) Matthew 25:1-13—In the parable of the ten virgins Jesus spoke of five foolish virgins typical of religiously deceived people. They possessed their lamps, which pictured religious ceremony. They made an outward profession of piety, symbolized by their robes. They had maintained their "religious virginity"—they were set apart unto religion. They even accompanied the wise virgins, which means they associated with those who were genuinely the children of God. Yet when they heard, "Behold, the bridegroom comes," they realized they could not enter the bridal chamber because they had no oil in their lamps. Their religion proved to be useless, being external only with no evidence of true spiritual life. They missed the kingdom of God.

b) 1 John—John wrote this epistle to affirm the faith of true believers and expose those who merely professed to be the children of God.

c) James—James pointedly addressed the issue of self-deception by giving a series of tests for true faith. He wanted the scattered Jews to whom he wrote to know the nature of their faith—whether legitimate or illegitimate.

Review

The three tests given by James are our response to trials (1:2-3), our response to temptations (1:12), and our response to the Word of God (1:19-27).

I. A PROPER RECEPTION OF THE WORD (vv. 19-21; see pp. 12-25)

   A. A Willingness to Receive the Word with Submission (vv. 19-20; see pp. 13-22)

   B. A Willingness to Receive the Word with Purity (v. 21a; see pp. 22-23)

   C. A Willingness to Receive the Word with Humility (v. 21b; see pp. 23-25)

II. A PROPER REACTION TO THE WORD (vv. 22-27; see pp. 34-43)

   A. A Willingness to Apply the Word Without Deception (vv. 36-43)

      1. The deception of hearing without responding (vv. 22b-25; see pp. 36-43)

Are You a Faithful Doer or a Self-Deceived Hearer?

I recently greeted a woman from another state who was visiting our church. I was pleased when she said, "Oh, Pastor, I so appreciated the message this morning. I saw what I must do in my life when you said we need to use our gifts for the Lord. When I go back to my home church I will begin to use the gifts that the Spirit of God has given me in service to Christ." I said, "Well, bless you. That's the response that encourages a preacher's heart and encourages the heart of God as well." The doer of the Word looks into the Word, sees the need, and acts on that need.

I believe a great number of professing Christians listen to the Word of God proclaimed and are involved in various religious activities but are destitute of the saving grace of God.

The second part of John Bunyan's *The Pilgrim's Progress* tells of Christiana and Mercy looking into a wonderful glass that was shown to them by the Shepherds of the Delectable Mountains. Bunyan wrote, "The glass was one of a thousand. It would present a man, one way, with his own features exactly; and turn it but another way, and it would show one the very face and similitude of the Prince of pilgrims himself. Yea, I have talked with them that can tell, and they have said that they have seen the very crown of thorns upon his head, by looking in that glass; they have therein also seen the holes in his hands, in his feet, and his side" ([New York: Pocket Books, 1957], p. 283).

When you look into the Word of God you'll see two things: your own sin and your Savior. The man who continues looking into the mirror of God's Word sees in it things far more wonderful than his own face. It's true that he sees the spots and stains in his life, but the longer he looks the clearer he sees the face of Jesus Christ, the Savior whose blood cleanses him from all his sin. The person who sees and responds to Christ by applying the Word to his life is blessed in doing so. Joshua 1:8 says, "This book of the law shall not depart out of thy mouth, but thou shalt meditate therein day and night, that thou mayest observe to do according to all that is written therein; for then thou shalt make thy way prosperous, and then thou shalt have good success." The doer of the Word habitually applies Scripture—anything less is self-deception.

Lesson

2. The deception of responding without exercising self-control (v. 26)

"If any man among you seem to be religious, and bridleth not his tongue, but deceiveth his own heart, this man's religion is in vain."

The person who hears the Word without responding is self-deceived. There is, however, another form of deception addressed by James—the deception of external religious activity without true internal purity of heart.

a) A wrong opinion

James says that such a person "seem to be religious." That implies a subjective mental opinion. It could be translated "he has the opinion of himself that he is religious" or "he thinks himself to be a religious person."

b) An uncontrolled tongue

James has previously made the point that if you are not doing the Word you may not really be saved (vv. 22-25). He now adds that if you are involved in religious activity but have not bridled your tongue, your religion is useless, no matter how evangelical or biblical it may be. It is a deception merely to go through the mechanics of reading the Bible, attending church, praying, giving money, or singing songs. The issue is a pure heart, and a pure heart is revealed by a controlled tongue. Of course one's speech is not all there is to Christian behavior, but it is an accurate indicator of the condition of one's heart. Jesus said, "Out of the abundance of the heart the mouth speaketh" (Matt. 12:34).

The Subtlety of Deception

Some people believe they are religious but are not true believers. They are not necessarily conscious of their hypocrisy. Their theology may be correct, they may be faithful churchgoers involved in various religious activities, and they may even be reinforced in their deception by undiscerning Christians who view them as true believers. Yet they have confused love of religious activity with love for God.

c) An external formality

The adjective translated "religious" (Gk., *thrēskos*, used also in vv. 26-27 in its noun form) has to do with ceremonial public worship. It was used, for example, by the Jewish historian Flavius Josephus when he wrote about worship in the Temple (K. L. Schmidt,

Theological Dictionary of the New Testament, s.v. *thrēs-kos*, ed. G. Kittel [Grand Rapids: Eerdmans, 1965], III:155-59). Paul uses it in Acts 26:5 in reference to the ceremonial worship of a Pharisee: "After the strictest sect of our religion I lived a Pharisee." In contrast, the Greek word *eusebia* refers to internal godliness of the heart. James used *thrēskos* to emphasize the externals of religious trappings, ceremonies, rituals, routines, liturgies, rites, and forms.

The point is this: If someone believes himself to be religious because he is involved in various rituals but does not demonstrate an inner control over his tongue, he is deceived and his religion is useless.

d) An unholy heart

Such a person "deceiveth his own heart" (v. 26). The English word *deceiveth* is derived from a Greek participle and is literally translated "if a man thinks himself to be religious while bridling not his tongue but deceiving his own heart." If he is unable to bridle his tongue, he is deceiving his own heart about the reality of his religion. Jesus said that corrupt speech betrays a corrupt heart (Matt. 12:33-35).

What Do Your Words Reveal About Your Heart?

Because the heart of a man is revealed in his words, you can learn much about a person's character if you listen long enough to what he says. James said, "If any man offend not in word, the same is a perfect man, and able also to bridle the whole body" (James 3:2). Jesus said, "By thy words thou shalt be justified, and by thy words thou shalt be condemned" (Matt. 12:37). A person who is outwardly religious yet has a tongue that is unbridled and out of control demonstrates a deceived and unholy heart.

e) A useless religion

If a person's tongue is not controlled, his heart is not transformed—no matter how many prayers he prays, how much biblical knowledge he has, or how many church activities he participates in. That's why James says, "This man's religion is vain" (v. 26).

The Greek word translated "vain" (*mataios*) means "futile," "useless," and "accomplishing nothing." It is frightening to realize that people can waste their lives in a religion that is vain, futile, and useless. The point is this: Religion that does not transform the heart accomplishes nothing.

A proper reaction to the Word is to receive it and apply it. Put the Word to work in your life. See the reality of your faith and do not be deceived. Allow God's Word to transform your heart and restrain your speech.

B. A Willingness to Apply the Word Without Selfishness (v. 27*a*)

"Pure religion and undefiled before God and the Father is this: to visit the fatherless and widows in their affliction."

1. The nature of true religion

True religion is demonstrating love and compassion toward orphans and widows amidst their difficulties. "Pure" and "undefiled" are synonyms used by James to indicate the purest kind of religion: showing compassionate love for one another. Jesus said, "By this shall all men know that ye are my disciples, if ye have love one to another" (John 13:35).

2. The judge of true religion

Pure and undefiled religion is measured by God according to His standard of love, not according to man's standard of external religious activity. You are genuinely religious when your life is marked by obedience to the Word and love toward others.

3. The activity of true religion

a) Explained

"To visit" means more than simply stopping by someone's home to give him a greeting. It carries the idea of bringing love, pity, and care to someone.

b) Exemplified

(1) Matthew 25:35-36—Jesus emphasized the priority of expressing compassion when He taught His disciples about the sheep and goat judgment. To the righteous He responded, "I was hungry, and ye gave me food; I was thirsty, and ye gave me drink; I was a stranger, and ye took me in; naked, and ye clothed me; I was sick, and ye visited me; I was in prison, and ye came unto me." That was not a superficial greeting but a loving provision of whatever was needed.

(2) 1 John 2:10-11—"He that loveth his brother abideth in the light, and there is no occasion of stumbling in him. But he that hateth his brother is in darkness, and walketh in darkness, and knoweth not where he goeth, because darkness hath blinded his eyes." The mark of a true believer is love for others.

(3) 1 John 3:10-18—"In this the children of God are manifest, and the children of the devil: whosoever doeth not righteousness is not of God, neither he that loveth not his brother. For this is the message that ye heard from the beginning, that we should love one another. Not as Cain, who was of that wicked one, and killed his brother. And why killed he him? Because his own works were evil, and his brother's righteous. Marvel not, my brethren, if the world hate you. We know that we have passed from death unto life, because we love the brethren. He that loveth not his brother abideth in death. Whosoever hateth his brother is a murderer; and ye know that no murderer hath eternal life abiding in him. By this perceive we the love of God, because he laid down his life for

us; and we ought to lay down our lives for the brethren. But whosoever hath this world's good, and seeth his brother have need, and shutteth up his compassions from him, how dwelleth the love of God in him? My little children, let us not love in word, neither in tongue, but in deed and in truth."

4. The recipients of true religion

   a) Explained

   Orphans and widows are an especially needy segment within the church. As the tongue represents the issue of a pure heart (v. 26), so widows and orphans represent the issue of pure love.

   b) Exemplified

   God has always been concerned about orphans and widows.

   (1) Exodus 22:22—"Ye shall not afflict any widow, or fatherless child."

   (2) Deuteronomy 14:28-29—Every third year a special tithe was collected from every Jewish person to care for the orphans, widows, and other needy people.

   (3) Deuteronomy 24:17-22—God had a profit-sharing plan for orphans and widows in the harvesting of all the fields.

   (4) Deuteronomy 27:19—God demanded justice for the orphan and widow.

   (5) Psalm 68:5—Why was God so attentive to the needs of orphans and widows? King David said, "A father of the fatherless, and a judge of the widows, is God in his holy habitation." God has a special place in His heart for people in great need.

(6) Jeremiah 7:6-7—"If ye oppress not the sojourner, the fatherless, and the widow, and shed not innocent blood in this place, neither walk after other gods to your harm; then will I cause you to dwell in this place, in the land that I gave to your fathers, forever and ever." God promised to bless the Israelites if they cared for widows and orphans.

(7) Acts 6:1-6—Proper care for widows was a concern of the early church, and they insured godly oversight of the matter.

(8) 1 Timothy 5:3—Paul told the church to "honor widows that are widows indeed"—to care for them financially. He followed that exhortation with a lengthy discussion on the proper care of widows (vv. 4-16).

Sacrificial Love: The Hallmark of True Christianity

Just as your speech reveals the condition of your heart, your attitude toward those in need reveals the genuineness of your love. Biblical love goes beyond those to whom we are attracted or with whom we share common interests. The apostle John said, "Beloved, let us love one another; for love is of God, and everyone that loveth is born of God, and knoweth God. He that loveth not knoweth not God; for God is love" (1 John 4:7-8). Our lives should be characterized by love, because true salvation is manifest through love. When we see people who are lonely, troubled, exploited, or in great physical need, yet we do not reach out to them in love and compassion, there is reason to question the genuineness of our Christianity. Unbelievers are predominantly committed to their own self-glory and self-indulgence. The redeemed reach out to others.

James reminds us that the proper way to receive the Word is with submission and humility. The proper reaction is to apply it without deception or selfishness.

C. A Willingness to Apply the Word Without Compromise (v. 27*b*)

"And to keep oneself unspotted from the world."

1. The exhortation

   The Greek word *kosmos* ("world") as used here refers to the evil world system in which we live. It includes the life-style, philosophy, morality, and ethics of our culture. "To keep oneself unspotted" means to continually keep oneself unstained by the filth and evil of the world. It is a simple and pointed exhortation.

2. The example

   Those of us who belong to God are to be like our Lord, described by Peter as "a lamb without blemish and without spot" (1 Pet. 1:19).

Taking Spiritual Inventory

John said, "Love not the world, neither the things that are in the world. If any man love the world, the love of the Father is not in him" (1 John 2:15). James added, "Ye adulterers and adulteresses, know ye not that the friendship of the world is enmity with God? Whosoever, therefore, will be a friend of the world is the enemy of God" (James 4:4). The two are incompatible. If you love the world, you do not love the Father. There is no place for compromise.

When you look at a person's life, do you see love for the world? Are his priorities and behavior governed by the life-style, philosophy, morality, and ethics of the evil culture in which he lives? If so, there is good reason to doubt his claim to Christianity. James says that pure religion belongs to people who show an inner control that is manifested in their speech, who show love for people in need, and who avoid being stained by the world. That's how a Christian lives.

When you look at your own life, do you see inconsistencies in your speech and in your love for others? What is your reaction at such times? The proof of your salvation is not found in the perfection of your life but in your reaction to your imperfections. Do you seek forgiveness and desire positive change? That is the reaction of a redeemed heart. Is the normal pattern of your speech that which is good, pure, honorable, truthful, and clean? Do you desire to honor God with everything you say? Such a desire rises out of a transformed heart.

What about the people in need? Does it trouble you to see folks who are deprived? Are you burdened to the point of helping when you can? Do you feel guilty when you fail to meet a need that you could have met? With regard to the world, is your heart repulsed and repentant when you find yourself beginning to conform to a worldly standard? Those are all marks of a transformed life.

Take spiritual inventory by asking yourself, *How do I know I am a Christian?* Here is the checklist James provided:

1. Your tongue. At the end of the day review the quality of your conversations. What does what you said reveal about the condition of your heart?

2. Your love for others. Is it your sincere desire to meet the needs of others? Do you receive great joy from helping those in need, or do you give simply to pacify your conscience or to make people think you are generous?

3. Your attitude toward the world. Do you want to win the world for Christ or be like the world? Do you want to get as much out of the world as you possibly can, or do you desire to remain untainted by it?

Your answer to those questions is an important indicator of the genuineness of your faith.

Conclusion

Pure religion is not a matter of external religious ceremony but of holy obedience flowing from an internal spiritual faith. It is not judged by man but by God Himself according to His standard. Although it is true "there is not a just man upon earth, that doeth good and sinneth not" (Eccles. 7:20), it is also true that "whosoever is born of God doth not [habitually] commit sin; for his seed remaineth in him, and he cannot [habitually] sin, because he is born of God" (1 John 3:9). Where there is habitual holy obedience there is true spiritual life.

Examine your life. Do you see a pattern of holy obedience? If so, you are a doer of the Word. Is your religion that which flows from a transformed heart, or is it nothing more than adherence to external religious ceremonies? How do you react to trials and temptations? How do you respond to the Word? True faith is a belief that behaves.

Focusing on the Facts

1. In the parable of the ten virgins, Jesus spoke of five wise and five foolish virgins. In what way were the five foolish virgins deceived, and what was the tragic result of their deception (Matt. 25:1-13; see p. 49)?
2. What two important results of looking intently into God's Word are illustrated in *The Pilgrim's Progress* (see p. 51)?
3. Explain the relationship between the content of one's speech and the condition of one's heart (see p. 52).
4. What is the nature of true religion (see p. 54)?
5. By whose standard is true religion judged, and what is that standard (see p. 54)?
6. Explain the meaning of the phrase "to visit" (v. 27; see pp. 55-56).
7. Why did James single out orphans and widows in his discussion of the practical expression of true religion (see p. 56)?
8. In what ways did God provide for orphans and widows in the Old Testament (see pp. 56-57)?
9. What is the responsibility of the church toward widows (1 Tim. 5:3-16; see p. 57)?
10. What is the hallmark of true Christianity (see p. 57)?
11. How are we to understand the usage of "world" in James 1:27 (see p. 58)?
12. What three areas did James give point to for taking spiritual inventory of our lives (see pp. 58-59)?

Pondering the Principles

1. The reality of spiritual deception is of such great concern to God that He repeatedly warns us not to fall victim to the subtle tactics of the enemy. Two classic examples of Satan's attempts at deception are recorded in Genesis 3:1-7 and Matthew 4:1-11. Read both passages carefully, making a comparison between the following aspects of each account.

   • Who is the tempter?
   • Who is being tempted?
   • Under what circumstances is the temptation taking place?
   • What is the motive of the tempter?
   • What is to be gained or lost by those being tempted if they overcome the temptation or are overcome by it?
   • What specific tactic(s) does Satan use in his attempts to deceive his victims?
   • Why did Eve fall victim to deception? How was Jesus able to be victorious?
   • How can I apply these insights to my life to help me avoid spiritual deception?

2. Review the section entitled "What Do Your Words Reveal About Your Heart?" (see p. 53). As you analyze the content of your speech, how do you judge your own heart? What impression does your speech make upon those who hear you? Unfortunately, many Christians genuinely love the Lord but are careless in what they say. Although their speech may not reveal an evil heart, it does reveal an insensitive heart. The following passages are given as a guide for Christian conversation: Ephesians 4:15, 25, 29; Colossians 4:6; Titus 2:1; 3:2; James 1:19; 4:11. Make a list of the principles taught in each passage. If you find yourself careless in any of the areas listed, ask the Lord to help you guard your speech.

3. James speaks of orphans and widows as representative of those within the church who have special needs. The Lord gives particular attention to meeting the needs of such people (see pp. 56-57), and we need to extend a hand of care and compassion to them as well. Is there someone in your family, church, or neighborhood who is in need? What can you do to help meet their

need? God doesn't require more than we can give, but He does ask us to share what we have.

4. Daniel is a wonderful example of a man who "kept himself unspotted from the world" (James 1:27). His success was rooted in an unwavering trust in the sovereignty of God and a clear understanding of God's purpose for his life (Dan. 2:19-23; 6:10). As you examine your own priorities, do you find them being influenced by the standards of the world? Remember, compromise is the first step toward defeat. Read Philippians 1:9-11. Ask God to strengthen the areas of your life in which you stand firm for the Lord and to reveal the areas in which there is subtle compromise. Pray daily for increased knowledge and discernment so that you may produce the fruit of righteousness and stand blameless before Him.

4
The Evil of Favoritism
in the Church—Part 1

Outline

Introduction
A. The Impartiality of God in the Old Testament
   1. 2 Chronicles 19:7
   2. Deuteronomy 10:17
   3. Malachi 2:9
B. The Impartiality of God in the New Testament
   1. With respect to salvation
   2. With respect to judgment
   3. With respect to employment status
   4. With respect to sin and discipline
   5. With respect to God's holy standard

Lesson
 I. The Principle (v. 1)
   A. Described
      1. The introduction (v. 1a)
      2. The problem (v. 1d)
      3. The command (v. 1b)
      4. The pattern (v. 1c)
   B. Demonstrated
II. The Example (vv. 2-4)
   A. The Setting (v. 2a)
   B. The Visitors (v. 2b)
      1. The rich man
         a) A gold ring
         b) Fine apparel
      2. The poor man

C. The Reception (v. 3)
   1. Of the rich man (v. 3*a*)
   2. Of the poor man (v. 3*b*)
D. The Sin (v. 4)

Conclusion

Introduction

The character of God is revealed in His attributes. One important attribute is His impartiality.

A. The Impartiality of God in the Old Testament

   1. 2 Chronicles 19:7—Jehoshaphat, king of Judah, said to his judges, "There is no iniquity with the Lord our God, nor respect of persons."

   2. Deuteronomy 10:17—Moses said to the people of Israel, "The Lord your God is God of gods and Lord of lords, the great God, mighty and awesome, who shows no partiality and accepts no bribes" (NIV).

   3. Malachi 2:9—The Lord said to the priests of Israel, "I also made you contemptible and base before all the people, according as ye have not kept my ways, but have been partial in the law." God judged the Israelite priests because they administered the law with partiality.

B. The Impartiality of God in the New Testament

   1. With respect to salvation

      When Peter presented the gospel to Gentiles, he acknowledged the impartiality of God in extending saving grace to people of every race: "Of a truth I perceive that God is no respecter of persons; but in every nation he that feareth him, and worketh righteousness, is accepted with him" (Acts 10:34-35).

2. With respect to judgment

Romans 2:9-11 says that God will bring "tribulation and anguish upon every soul of man that doeth evil, of the Jew first, and also of the Greek; but glory, honor, and peace, to every man that worketh good, to the Jew first, and also to the Greek; for there is no respect of persons with God."

3. With respect to employment status

The employment status of an individual is inconsequential to the Lord. He doesn't have greater love for a manager, president, vice-president, executive, or boss than He does for the humblest of all servants (cf. Col. 3:22–4:1). Paul warned masters to treat their servants with fairness and dignity, "knowing that [their] Master also is in heaven; neither is there respect of persons with him" (Eph. 6:9).

4. With respect to sin and discipline

Paul warned Timothy, saying, "Against an elder receive not an accusation, but before two or three witnesses. Them that sin rebuke before all, that others also may fear. I charge thee before God, and the Lord Jesus Christ, and the elect angels, that thou observe these things without preferring one before another, doing nothing by partiality" (1 Tim. 5:19-21).

5. With respect to God's holy standard

Peter said, "Be ye holy; for I am holy. And if ye call on the Father, who without respect of persons judgeth according to every man's work, pass the time of your sojourning here in fear" (1 Pet. 1:16-17). The holiness of God as manifested in righteous deeds will be the standard by which men will be judged.

We are prone to judge one another on the basis of external considerations, but God is not interested in such things. The Lord reminded Samuel that "man looketh on the outward appearance, but the Lord looketh on the heart" (1 Sam. 16:7). As His children we should manifest that same impartiality.

Moses warned the judges of Israel to avoid partiality in the exercise of their responsibilities: "Ye shall not respect persons in judgment, but ye shall hear the small as well as the great; ye shall not be afraid of the face of man, for the judgment is God's; and the cause that is too hard for you, bring it unto me, and I will hear it" (Deut. 1:17). He also said, "Thou shalt not respect persons, neither take a bribe; for a bribe doth blind the eyes of the wise and pervert the words of the righteous" (Deut. 16:19).

Israel was to treat its poor with fairness regardless of their social status: "If there be among you a poor man of one of thy brethren within any of thy gates in thy land which the Lord thy God giveth thee, thou shalt not harden thine heart, nor shut thine hand from thy poor brother; but thou shalt open thine hand wide unto him, and shalt surely lend him sufficient for his need, in that which he lacketh. Beware that there be not a thought in thy wicked heart, saying, The seventh year, the year of release, is at hand; and thine eye be evil against thy poor brother, and thou givest him nothing; and he cry unto the Lord against thee, and it be sin unto thee. Thou shalt surely give him, and thine heart shall not be grieved when thou givest unto him, because for this thing the Lord thy God shall bless thee in all thy works, and in all that thou puttest thine hand unto. For the poor shall never cease out of the land; therefore I command thee, saying, Thou shalt open thine hand wide unto thy brother, to thy poor, and to thy needy, in thy land" (Deut. 15:7-11).

The counsel of Solomon is consistent with that of Moses: "It is not good to have respect of persons in judgment" (Prov. 24:23; cf. Prov. 28:21).

The book of James gives a series of tests for living faith. So far we've looked at how we respond to trials, temptation, and the Word of God. Another test is our reaction to the poor and needy. The apostle John wrote, "By this perceive we the love of God, because he laid down his life for us; and we ought to lay down our lives for the brethren. But whosoever hath this world's good, and seeth his brother have need, and shutteth up his compassions from him, how dwelleth the love of God in him?" (1 John 3:16-17). First John 4:10-12 says, "Herein is love, not that we loved God, but that he loved us, and sent his Son to be the propitiation for our sins. Beloved, if God so loved us, we ought also to love one another. No man hath seen God at any time. If we love one another, God dwelleth in us, and his love is perfected in us." If we claim to possess the love of God, our response to those in need should be consistent with His response to us. The godly person will avoid favoritism.

Lesson

James 2:1-13 conveys five features relative to favoritism within the church: the principle (v. 1), the example (vv. 2-4), the inconsistency (vv. 5-7), the violation (vv. 8-11), and the appeal (vv. 12-13).

I. THE PRINCIPLE (v. 1)

"My brethren, have not the faith of our Lord Jesus Christ, the Lord of glory, with respect of persons."

Claiming to hold to the faith of Jesus Christ while practicing partiality is contradictory.

The Poor in the Early Church

The greatest number of Christian converts in the early church were poor. Celsus, a dabbler in Platonic philosophy, wrote a diatribe against Christianity in approximately A.D. 178. He portrayed Christians as uncultured and ignorant, saying they were uneducated, vulgar, and common (Origen, *Against Celsus* 6.12-15). Although unkind, his words reflect one perception of the social makeup of the early church. Scripture gives abundant evidence for the presence of poor people in the church.

1. Acts 4:13—Luke recorded the reaction of the Jewish religious leaders to the preaching of Peter and John: "When they saw the boldness of Peter and John, and perceived that they were un-

learned and ignorant men, they marveled; and they took knowledge of them, that they had been with Jesus."

2. Acts 2:44-45—"All that believed were together, and had all things common; and sold their possessions and goods, and parted them to all men, as every man had need." Those who had land or houses sold many of their possessions and brought the money to the apostles for distribution to the poor (Acts 4:35-37).

3. Acts 6:1-8—The first problem in the church arose out of concern for the needs of poor widows.

4. 1 Corinthians 1:26-28—Paul said, "Ye see your calling, brethren, how that not many wise men after the flesh, not many mighty, not many noble, are called; but God hath chosen the foolish things of the world to confound the wise; and God hath chosen the weak things of the world to confound the things which are mighty; and base things of the world, and things which are despised, hath God chosen, yea, and things which are not, to bring to nothing things that are." By the world's standards, there aren't many mighty, noble, or wise people within the ranks of Christianity—merely the common people.

5. James 2:5—"Hath not God chosen the poor of this world to be rich in faith and heirs of the kingdom which he hath promised to them that love him?" The majority of the church has always been poor, common people.

Although the majority of believers were poor, there were exceptions.

1. Matthew 27:57-60—Joseph of Arimathea provided for the burial of Christ. He was described as "a rich man" (v. 57).

2. Acts 4:34-37—There were believers in the early church who were property owners.

3. Acts 8:27—The Ethiopian eunuch was a man of high rank and great authority under Candace, queen of the Ethiopians.

4. Acts 10:1—Cornelius, the first recorded Gentile convert, was a Roman centurion and a man of some means.

5. Acts 13:7—Sergius Paulus was a high ranking official on the isle of Cyprus who desired to hear the Word of God from Barnabas and Paul. He "believed, being astonished at the doctrine of the Lord" (v. 12).

6. Acts 16:14—Lydia, a convert from the city of Thyatira, was a seller of purple cloth, so she operated her own business.

7. Acts 17:4—As Paul preached at Thessalonica, many people believed, including some prominent women of the city.

8. Acts 18:1-3—Priscilla and Aquila had their own tentmaking business.

Although there were people of means within the early church, the majority of people were poor. At times it was necessary for the church to provide organized funding and relief for the poor. During one severe famine, "the disciples, every man according to his ability, determined to send relief unto the brethren who dwelt in Judaea; which also they did, and sent it to the elders by the hands of Barnabas and Saul" (Acts 11:29-30). The churches of Macedonia, who were extremely poor themselves, gave abundantly to the poor saints at Jerusalem (2 Cor. 8:1-2). The mixture of rich and poor within the church gave opportunity for the rich to give to the poor, but it also presented the potential for sinful stratification based upon social standing and economic capability. Such stratification is inconsistent with godliness.

A. Described

James 2:1 says, "My brethren, have not the faith of our Lord Jesus Christ, the Lord of glory, with respect of persons." The Greek text is literally translated, "My brothers, with respect of persons, do not hold the faith of our Lord Jesus Christ, the glory."

1. The introduction (v. 1a)

"My brethren."

James often used the phrase "my brethren" to introduce a new and forceful exhortation. For example, in 1:2 he says, "My brethren," then exhorts his readers about trials and temptations. In 1:16 he says, "Do not err, my beloved brethren," then speaks about a proper response to the Word of God. In 2:1, our text under consideration, he introduces the need for impartiality. In 3:1 he uses "my brethren" to begin a discussion about the tongue. In 4:11 he says, "Speak not evil of one another, brethren," then exhorts them toward proper speech. And in 5:7 he uses the phrase in exhorting them to be patient for the coming of the Lord.

2. The problem (v. 1*d*)

"Respect of persons."

The Greek word translated "respect" is a plural word meaning "partialities." In our fallenness we tend to judge people by external criteria such as looks, clothing, place of residence, or economic situation. All such partiality is contrary to true faith.

3. The command (v. 1*b*)

"Hold not the faith of our Lord Jesus Christ . . . with respect of persons."

That is an imperative command: Don't practice partiality. Don't claim to be a Christian while at the same time acting partial.

God Looks at the Heart

A person's true worth is based upon the value of his soul. God looks beyond any external considerations and sees into the heart of an individual. That is where true evaluation must take place. Anything less can lead to sinful favoritism. James 2:9 says, "If ye have respect of persons, ye commit sin, and are convicted of the law as transgressors." Our behavior must reflect the impartiality of God.

Is it showing partiality to honor to those in authority over us? No. Scripture instructs us to do so (cf. 1 Pet. 2:17; Rom. 13:1). Giving honor to those in authority is biblical; showing partiality against those whom we disapprove of is sinful.

4. The pattern (v. 1c)

"The Lord of glory."

In the Greek text James ended his exhortation with the apposition "the glory" (Gk., *doxa*), which speaks of Christ as the glory of God revealed. Jesus' divine glory was veiled in human flesh. He took on our nature, bore our sin, and took our curse. Jesus reflected God's impartial nature. Even His enemies recognized that: "Then went the Pharisees, and took counsel how they might entangle [Jesus] in his talk. And they sent out unto him their disciples with the Herodians, saying, Master, we know that thou art true, and teachest the way of God in truth, neither carest thou for any man; for thou regardest not the person of men" (Matt. 22:15-16). To Jesus the worth of the individual was based upon the worth of his soul.

The impartiality of Jesus is further seen in the promise that "we shall be like him; for we shall see him as he is" (1 John 3:2). He will make each of us like Himself. In addition, we will all receive the same eternal reward (Matt. 19:30–20:16). How then can we who claim to hold the faith of the Lord Jesus Christ, the glorious God incarnate, justify treating others with partiality? You cannot uphold the faith of Jesus Christ while violating the nature of God with your partiality.

B. Demonstrated (discussed in the next chapter on pp. 79-81)

II. THE EXAMPLE (vv. 2-4)

A. The Setting (v. 2a)

"If there come unto your assembly."

James used a third class conditional clause in the Greek text to indicate the possibility of his hypothetical illustration coming to pass. The word translated "assembly" is *sunagōgē* (lit., "a gathering together"), from which we get our English word *synagogue*. The more common word for the Christian assembly is *ekklēsia*, which James used in 5:14: "Is any sick among you? Let him call for the elders of the church." However, the Jewish believers to whom James wrote had a special appreciation of *sunagōgē* as a reference to the assembly of God's people. The setting, therefore, is the believers' church meeting.

B. The Visitors (v. 2*b*)

"A man with a gold ring, in fine apparel, and . . . a poor man in vile raiment."

A literal translation of the Greek text conveys a vivid picture: "If there come into your synagogue a gold-fingered man in shining bright apparel and there come in also a poor man in shabby clothes."

1. The rich man

   a) A gold ring

   In ancient Jewish culture, rings were commonly worn by both men and women. When the prodigal son returned home (Luke 15:11-32), his father said to the servants, "Bring forth the best robe, and put it on him; and put a ring on his hand, and shoes on his feet" (v. 22). Although rings were common, only the wealthy could afford gold rings. Commentator William Barclay tells us there were businesses where people could rent rings to wear when they wished to give an impression of great wealth (*The Letters of James and Peter* [Philadelphia: Westminster, 1976], p. 64). On the other hand, the third-century Greek theologian Clement of Alexandria advised teachers that a Christian man should wear only one ring and that he should wear it on his little finger. Its main purpose was to be used as a seal or a stamp and was to bear the emblem of a dove, fish, ship, musical lyre, or anchor

(*The Ante-Nicene Fathers*, vol. 2, trans. Alexander Roberts and James Donaldson [Grand Rapids: Eerdmans, 1975], pp. 285-86).

b) Fine apparel

The word translated "fine" (Gk., *lampros*) apparel speaks of loud colors and that which is glittering and brilliant with ornamentation. It is the term used of the gorgeous apparel that the soldiers put on Jesus to mock Him (Luke 23:11) and the shining garments of the angel who appeared to Cornelius in Acts 10:30. The picture James paints is of a rich man entering the assembly with gold rings and flashy clothing. Note that the dress of the rich man is not the issue in this passage. He is not required to change clothing, neither is he condemned for his dress. The issue is the motives of those who welcome him to the assembly.

2. The poor man

The word translated "poor" (Gk., *ptōchos*) is the word for abject poverty. This person was a beggar at the lowest level of society. The Greek word translated "vile" means "filthy," "smelly," "dirty," or "shabby." Undoubtedly this poor beggar owned only one robe, in which he slept, sweat, worked, and lived. His appearance was in stark contrast to that of the rich man. However, as with the rich man, the dress of the poor man is not the issue in this passage.

C. The Reception (v. 3)

1. Of the rich man (v. 3*a*)

"Ye have respect to him that weareth the fine clothing, and say unto him, Sit thou here in a good place."

In this context to respect means to look upon someone with favor or attention. That man attracted everyone's attention, and they gave him preferential treatment so they could win his favor or perhaps profit from his wealth.

There were few benches in the synagogues and assembly halls of that day. Perhaps a few lined the outer wall or were in the front of the assembly. Most people had to choose between standing or sitting cross-legged on the floor. To be offered a seat was special. Offering a prominent seat to a guest is not a sinful act if motivated by courtesy and hospitality. However, the sinfulness of this situation is revealed in the reception given to the poor man.

2. Of the poor man (v. 3b)

"And say to the poor, Stand thou there, or sit here under my footstool."

The word translated "under" (Gk., *hupo*) could be translated "beside." If the reference is to a literal footstool, someone in the assembly had both a chair and a footstool, and he wouldn't give either to the poor man.

Why was the poor man treated unkindly, whereas the rich man was given preferential treatment? Because there is something built into our fallenness that is partial to people who look nice, smell pleasant, and are wealthy. Such partiality is at the heart of the sin that James is exposing.

D. The Sin (v. 4)

"Are ye not then partial in yourselves, and are become judges with evil thoughts?"

To act with partiality is to make distinctions, separations, divisions, or discriminations. It is showing favoritism based upon unimportant external criteria. All such behavior is serious sin because it violates the nature of God. The Greek word translated "evil" means "vicious." When you show partiality you are behaving like the sinful world. You are catering to the rich and prominent while shunning the poor and common. Such behavior is anti-Christian and has no place in the church of God.

Conclusion

The book of Romans concludes with this thought: "The God of patience and consolation grant you to be like-minded one toward another according to Christ Jesus, that ye may with one mind and one mouth glorify God, even the Father of our Lord Jesus Christ. Wherefore, receive ye one another, as Christ also received us to the glory of God" (15:5-7). We are to receive one another with the same impartiality with which Christ received us. It is not sinful to have wealth if God has prospered you, and it is not wrong to have little. God makes no distinctions on such things, and neither should we. If we show favoritism we are not acting in a godly way but have become judges with vicious intents.

Focusing on the Facts

1. How did the Israelite priests violate the impartiality of God, and what was the outcome (Mal. 2:9; see p. 64)?
2. In what way did Peter's preaching to Cornelius demonstrate the impartiality of God (Acts 10:34-35; see p. 64)?
3. What will be the criterion upon which God will judge a man (Rom. 2:9-11; see p. 65)?
4. How does God compare the worth of a common laborer with that of a corporation president (Col. 3:22–4:1; see p. 65)?
5. What is God's perspective on the importance of external considerations? In light of His perspective, how should Christians behave toward people of varying economic situations (see pp. 65-66)?
6. What warnings did Moses give to the judges of Israel about showing partiality (Deut. 1:17; 16:19; see p. 66)?
7. According to the apostle John, what is the relationship between love for God and man (1 John 3:16-17; 4:10-12; see p. 67)?
8. What do we learn from Celsus about the social status of most early Christians (see p. 67)? Is his perception supported or denied by Scripture (see pp. 67-68)?
9. Were all early Christians poor? What biblical evidence can you cite in support of your answer (see pp. 68-69)?
10. How did James use the introduction "my brethren" (see pp. 69-70)?

11. Explain what it means to have "respect of persons" (v. 1; see p. 70).
12. What did James mean by "the Lord of glory" (v. 1; see p. 71)?
13. Read James 2:2. Contrast the dress of the rich man with that of the poor man (see pp. 72-73).
14. What was the response of the assembly to the rich man? To the poor man? What made their responses sinful (v. 3; see pp. 73-74)?
15. What is the sin of partiality (v. 4; see p. 74)?
16. Define "evil" as used in James 2:4 (see p. 74).

Pondering the Principles

1. The story is told of a pastor who kept an updated copy of all-church members' contributions to help him determine his level of availability should one of them require his services. Although we may react with great indignation to such an obvious display of favoritism, we too must guard our hearts carefully lest we fall victim to its subtle influence. One way of cultivating an impartial heart is by reflecting often upon the impartial character of God. Review the sections on the impartiality of God in the Old and New Testaments (see pp. 64-66). Then set aside some time to meditate on Psalm 33, which reflects on God's righteousness and justice. Spend time in prayer praising God for His righteous character, creative power, and gracious provisions to all who fear Him.

2. Have you ever experienced rejection as a result of the partiality of others? How did you feel? What was your response? Paul spoke directly to that issue when he said to the Roman Christians, "Accept one another, just as Christ also accepted us to the glory of God" (Rom. 15:7, NASB*). Read Romans 12:16 and James 2:1-4, and make a note of the causes of partiality. Do you see any trace of those elements in your life? Read Romans 12:3-5, 15:7, and Philippians 2:1-5. What remedies for partiality does Paul give? Endeavor to apply those remedies to your life.

*New American Standard Bible.

5
The Evil of Favoritism
in the Church—Part 2

Outline

Introduction

Review
I. The Principle (v. 1)
   A. The Principle Described

Lesson
   B. The Principle Demonstrated
      1. The Lord's genealogy
      2. The Lord's residence
      3. The Lord's ministry
      4. The Lord's teachings
         a) Matthew 20:1-16
         b) Matthew 22:1-14
         c) Mark 12:38-44
         d) Luke 5:32
II. The Example (vv. 2-4)
III. The Inconsistency (vv. 5-7)
   A. The Divine Choice of the Poor (vv. 5-6a)
      1. The identity of the poor
      2. God's affection for the poor
         a) As seen in the Old Testament
         b) As seen in the New Testament
            (1) The rich young ruler (Matt. 19:16-26)
            (2) Zacchaeus (Luke 19:1-10)
            (3) Judas (John 12:1-6)
            (4) Paul (Gal. 2:9-10)

Introduction

Throughout his epistle, James gave a series of tests for true Christian faith: a proper response to trials, temptation, the Word of God, and those in need. In James 2:1-13 he presents one's response to partiality as another test of true faith.

The problem of partiality in the church extended far beyond the congregation to which James wrote. The apostle John confronted the same issue when he wrote, "We love him, because he first loved us. If a man says, I love God, and hateth his brother, he is a liar; for he that loveth not his brother, whom he hath seen, how can he love God, whom he hath not seen? And this commandment have we from him, that he who loveth God love his brother also" (1 John 4:19-21). Repeatedly John said that the quality of one's love for others reveals the quality of his faith in God. If we judge one another by unimportant external criteria, we have sinned, and our love for God is suspect.

Review

I. THE PRINCIPLE (v. 1; see pp. 67-71, 79-81)

  A. The Principle Described (see pp. 69-71)

B. The Principle Demonstrated

You cannot practice partiality and be consistent with the example of Jesus Christ, who is the revelation of the divine, impartial character of God. Various aspects of His life demonstrate His impartiality.

1. The Lord's genealogy

The genealogy of Jesus (Matt. 1:1-17; Luke 3:23-38) includes Tamar, who committed incest; Rahab, who was a prostitute; Ruth, who was an idolater; and Bathsheba, who was the adulterous paramour of David. It also includes godly people and people from all levels of society.

2. The Lord's residence

Jesus was born in Bethlehem, the city of David. But after a brief sojourn in Egypt, His family settled in the Galilean town of Nazareth (Matt. 2:13-23). It was a common man's town about which was asked, "Can any good thing come out of Nazareth?" (John 1:46). Peter and John were also from the region of Galilee and were thought by the Jewish leaders to be "unlearned and ignorant men" (Acts 4:13). Such was the reputation of Galileans.

3. The Lord's ministry

The majority of our Lord's ministry took place among those who had little or no material resources.

4. The Lord's teachings

Throughout His ministry Jesus taught the principles of impartiality.

a) Matthew 20:1-16—Jesus told a story about a landowner who hired several groups of men to harvest his grapes. At six A.M. he hired the first group of men who, at the end of the day, had worked a total of twelve hours. The last group of men worked only one hour. Even though each group worked different lengths of time, at the end of the day each man was paid the same amount: one denarius. Jesus was illustrating the principle that "the last shall be first, and the first last" (v. 16). As it relates to the kingdom of God, everyone will end up in a tie. No matter who you are or how long you have served, all who love God will receive the same thing—eternal life. What a wonderful promise!

b) Matthew 22:1-14—Jesus told a parable about the marriage of a king's son, a reference to Christ. When the wedding arrangements were complete, the invited guests (Israel) did not show up. The king therefore said to his servants, "Go, therefore, into the highways, and as many as ye shall find [Jew or Gentile], bid to the marriage" (v. 9). There was no discrimination or partiality in his directive. His servants obeyed by going "out . . . and [gathering] together all, as many as they found, both bad and good; and the wedding was furnished with guests" (v. 10). The wedding was furnished with all types of people —moral and immoral, religious and irreligious, family people and street people—all types. When it comes to calling people to Himself, Jesus is absolutely impartial. In fact, the only requirement for salvation is to acknowledge yourself to be a sinner in need of His saving grace.

c) Mark 12:38-44—Jesus warned the common people to "beware of the scribes, who love to go in long clothing, and love salutations in the market places, and the chief seats in the synagogues, and the uppermost places at feasts; who devour widows' houses, and for a pretense make long prayers; these shall receive greater condemnation" (vv. 38-40). He then went on to illustrate His impartiality as He "sat opposite the treasury, and beheld how the people cast money into the treasury; and many that were rich cast in much. And there came a certain poor widow, and she threw in two mites, which make a farthing. And he called unto him his disciples, and said unto them, Verily I say unto you, This poor widow hath cast more in than all they who have cast into the treasury; for all they did cast in of their abundance, but she of her want did cast in all that she had, even all her living" (vv. 41-44). Jesus was unimpressed with displays of religious devotion devoid of any true commitment. He evaluated people solely upon the openness of their hearts and their willingness to respond in faith to the message He proclaimed.

d) Luke 5:32—Jesus summed up His ministry when He said, "I came not to call the righteous, but sinners to repentance."

If you are committed to faith in Christ you must be committed to impartiality.

II. THE EXAMPLE (vv. 2-4; see pp. 71-75, 81-82)

The Gospel Is the Great Equalizer

James 1:9-10 says, "Let the brother of low degree rejoice in that he is exalted; but the rich, in that he is made low, because as the flower of the grass he shall pass away." The gospel is the great equalizer. It takes the poor man and exalts him to heavenly riches and strips the rich man of vain earthly riches.

Although it is necessary to judge between such things as truth and error, right and wrong, God forbids arbitrary favoritism. If we bear the name of God, we must not discriminate on the basis of things that are insignificant in His sight. Such behavior contradicts the Christian faith at its very core.

Consider the example of Jesus, who, "though he was rich, yet for your sakes he became poor, that ye through his poverty might be rich" (2 Cor. 8:9). Jesus extended the wonderful offer of salvation to everyone, saying, "Come unto me, all ye that labor and are heavy laden, and I will give you rest. Take my yoke upon you, and learn of me; for I am meek and lowly in heart, and ye shall find rest unto your souls. For my yoke is easy, and my burden is light" (Matt. 11:28-30).

The gospel is the great equalizer. Anyone who seeks forgiveness is invited to come to Jesus. Impartiality is the essence of our Lord's nature. If we act contrary to His example, we are acting as judges with evil, discriminatory motives.

III. THE INCONSISTENCY (vv. 5-7)

"Hearken, my beloved brethren, Hath not God chosen the poor of this world to be rich in faith and heirs of the kingdom which he hath promised to them that love him? But ye have despised the poor. Do not rich men oppress you, and draw you before the judgment seats? Do not they blaspheme that worthy name by the which ye are called?"

The way James called the attention of his readers ("hearken, my beloved brethren") reveals his love for his readers and his concern for the truth. His point is this: To be partial to the rich and turn your back on the poor is inconsistent in light of the divine choice of the poor (v. 5) and the blasphemy of the rich (v. 7). When you side with the rich, you side with the blasphemers. When you go against the poor and the downcast, you go against the ones God has chosen.

A. The Divine Choice of the Poor (vv. 5-6a)

"Hearken, my beloved brethren, Hath not God chosen the poor of this world to be rich in faith and heirs of the kingdom which he hath promised to them that love him? But ye have despised the poor."

When you show partiality you are despising the very ones God has chosen.

1. The identity of the poor

The poor James refers to are not those who are "poor in spirit" (Matt. 5:3). He was speaking about those who are poor in the eyes of the world—those who don't have the necessities of life.

Not All the Elect Are Poor

Generally speaking, the elect of God are predominantly the poor. However, not all the elect are poor.

1. Abraham

Abraham was an extremely wealthy man. Genesis 13:2 says he "was very rich in cattle, in silver, and in gold." God had prospered him and chosen him to be the father of the Jewish nation.

2. Job

Job had "seven thousand sheep, and three thousand camels, and five hundred yoke of oxen, and five hundred she-asses, and a very great household; so that this man was the greatest of all the men of the east" (Job 1:3). Job was a wealthy man who was uniquely godly. God literally turned Satan loose to test him.

3. Joseph of Arimathea

The wealth of Joseph of Arimathea was such that he could provide a garden tomb for the burial of the Lord Jesus Christ (Matt. 27:57-60; John 19:38-42).

4. Matthew

Levi, who later became known as Matthew, was a tax collector (Luke 5:27-35). Tax collectors were wealthy because of their infamous corruption.

5. Zacchaeus

Zacchaeus was the chief tax collector, which probably meant that he was not only collecting money for himself, but also was getting a portion of what was collected by the other tax collectors. He had parlayed his income into such wealth that he could repay those whom he had cheated four times what he had taken from them (Luke 19:8).

6. Others

There were other rich believers within the early church. Paul instructed Timothy to "charge them that are rich in this age, that they be not high-minded, nor trust in uncertain riches but in the living God, who giveth us richly all things to enjoy; that they do good, that they be rich in good works, ready to distribute, willing to share, laying up in store for themselves a good foundation against the time to come, that they may lay hold on eternal life" (1 Tim. 6:17-19).

2. God's affection for the poor

a) As seen in the Old Testament

(1) Psalm 41:1-3—"Blessed is he that considereth the poor; the Lord will deliver him in time of trouble. The Lord will preserve him, and keep him alive; and he shall be blessed upon the earth, and thou wilt not deliver him unto the will of his enemies. The Lord will strengthen him upon the bed of languishing; thou wilt make all his bed in his sickness." If you take care of the poor, God will take care of you.

(2) Psalm 68:10—"Thou, O God, hast prepared of thy goodness for the poor."

(3) Psalm 72:4—"He shall judge the poor of the people, he shall save the children of the needy, and shall break in pieces the oppressor." God is the defender of the poor. He meets their needs and goes after their enemies.

(4) Psalm 72:12-13—"He shall deliver the needy when he crieth; the poor also, and him that hath no helper. He shall spare the poor and needy, and shall save the souls of the needy." The tendency of rich people is to attempt to solve their problems with their own resources, whereas out of their desperation the poor often cry out for divine assistance.

(5) Psalm 113:7—"He raiseth up the poor out of the dust, and lifteth the needy out of the dunghill." God exalts the poor.

(6) Proverbs 17:5—"Whoso mocketh the poor reproacheth his Maker." When you mock a poor man, treat him with disdain, or fail to meet his need, you mock God.

(7) Proverbs 21:13—"Whoso stoppeth his ears at the cry of the poor, he also shall cry himself, but shall not be heard." If your prayers aren't being answered, you might do an inventory and see if you have stopped your ears to the needs of someone around you.

(8) Proverbs 28:27—"He that giveth unto the poor shall not lack, but he that hideth his eyes shall have many a curse." God will provide for those who give to the poor.

(9) Proverbs 29:7—"The righteous considereth the cause of the poor, but the wicked regardeth not to know it." The wicked man doesn't want to know about the needs of the poor.

(10) Proverbs 31:9—"Plead the cause of the poor and needy."

(11) Proverbs 31:20—The godly woman "stretcheth out her hand to the poor; yea, she reacheth forth her hands to the needy." She has the heart of God.

(12) Isaiah 3:14-15—"The Lord will enter into judgment with the ancients of his people, and their princes; for ye have eaten up the vineyard; the spoil of the poor is in your houses. What mean ye that ye beat my people to pieces, and grind the faces of the poor? saith the Lord God of hosts." Be careful how you treat poor people.

(13) Isaiah 10:1-3—"Woe unto them who decree unrighteous decrees, and who write grievousness

which they have prescribed, to turn aside the needy from justice, and to take away the right from the poor of my people, that widows may be their prey, and that they may rob the fatherless! And what will ye do in the day of visitation, and in the desolation which shall come from afar? To whom will ye flee for help? And where will ye leave your glory?" God is saying, "What are you going to do when I come after you for the way you've treated the poor?"

(14) Isaiah 25:1-4—"O Lord . . . thou hast been a strength to the poor, a strength to the needy in his distress, a refuge from the storm, a shadow from the heat, when the blast of the terrible ones is like a storm against the wall." The Lord helps people who are in distress. He reaches out to the poor, to those in great need. It is His character to do so. How can those who profess to be His children do any less?

(15) Amos 2:6—"Thus saith the Lord: For three transgressions of Israel, and for four, I will not turn away its punishment, because they sold the righteous for silver, and the poor for a pair of shoes." God condemned Israel because they sinned against the poor people (4:1; 5:11-12). The nation of Israel continually needed to repent of the sin of mistreatment of the poor.

God's Provision for the Poor

In the Old Testament God provided for poor people in several ways.

1. The sacrificial system (Lev. 5:7)—God provided for the offering of a turtledove or pigeon if the worshiper could not afford a lamb.

2. The Sabbath year (Deut. 15:1-23)—Every seventh year was the Sabbath year of the land. The poor people had all their debts canceled so that they wouldn't have to go deeper and deeper into debt.

3. The Jubilee year (Lev. 25:8-55)—All the slaves were given their freedom after seven Sabbath years (forty-nine years).

4. A share in the harvest (Lev. 19:9-10)—The Israelites were instructed by God to leave the corners of the field unharvested so that the poor could gather food from that portion of the field.

5. Interest-free loans (Lev. 25:35-37)—God forbade charging interest to poor people. They were to be given the money they needed, or given an interest-free loan. Anything else was considered usury (exorbitant interest) and was severely punished by God.

6. Redemption from debt (Lev. 25:25)—If a poor person got into debt, a brother could redeem him by paying his debt.

7. Employment by a neighbor (Lev. 25:39-40)—When a poor person was out of a job, his nearest neighbor was to employ him.

If we say we walk with the God who chose "the poor of this world to be rich in faith and heirs of the kingdom" (James 2:5), we will share His concern for such people. The quality of our love for God will be revealed in our attitude toward the poor. James said, "Pure religion and undefiled . . . is to visit the fatherless and widows" (James 1:27).

    b) As seen in the New Testament

        (1) The rich young ruler (Matt. 19:16-26)—In response to the young ruler's question, "What good thing shall I do, that I may have eternal life?" (v. 16), Jesus essentially said, "Let Me test whether you're willing to follow Me: take everything you have, sell it, and give the money to the poor" (v. 21). However, the ruler went away "sorrowful; for he had great possessions" (v. 22). His claim to have kept the entire law (v. 20) was refuted by his unwillingness to love his neighbor as himself (v. 19). A heart set upon God is a heart set upon meeting the needs of others.

        (2) Zacchaeus (Luke 19:1-10)—When this notorious tax collector was converted he said to Jesus, "Behold, Lord, the half of my goods I give to the

poor; and if I have taken anything from any man by false accusation, I restore him fourfold" (v. 8). Suddenly the heart of God was controlling Zacchaeus. As a result Jesus said to him, "This day is salvation come to this house" (v. 9). The evidence of true salvation was an attitude of mercy toward the poor and a desire to make restitution for past sins.

(3) Judas (John 12:1-6)—"Jesus, six days before the passover, came to Bethany, where Lazarus was, who had been dead, whom he raised from the dead. There they made him a supper, and Martha served; but Lazarus was one of them that sat at the table with him. Then took Mary a pound of ointment of spikenard, very costly, and anointed the feet of Jesus, and wiped his feet with her hair; and the house was filled with the odor of the ointment. Then saith one of his disciples, Judas Iscariot, Simon's son, who should betray him, Why was not this ointment sold for three hundred denarii, and given to the poor? This he said, not that he cared for the poor, but because he was a thief, and had the bag, and bore what was put in it." Jesus and the disciples probably gave often to the poor (cf. John 13:29). Judas gave evidence of never being converted because he cared only for his own pocket, not for the needs of the poor. The kind of love that reaches out to the poor is a mark of true salvation.

(4) Paul (Gal. 2:9-10)—Paul said, "[The Jerusalem church] gave to me and Barnabas the right hands of fellowship, that we should go unto the Gentiles, and they unto the circumcision. Only they would that we should remember the poor; the same which I also was diligent to do." When Paul was commissioned to preach the gospel, he was exhorted to remember the poor. Romans 15:25-26 illustrates that he was faithful in fulfilling that commission: "I go unto Jerusalem to minister unto the saints. For it hath pleased them of Macedonia and Achaia to make a certain contribution for the poor saints who are at Jerusalem."

c) As seen in His calling of Israel

Moses said to the Israelites, "The Lord did not set his love upon you, nor choose you, because ye were more in number than any people; for ye were the fewest of all people. But because the Lord loved you, and because he would keep the oath which he had sworn unto your fathers, hath the Lord brought you out with a mighty hand, and redeemed you out of the house of bondage, from the hand of Pharaoh, king of Egypt" (Deut. 7:7-8). God saw them in their distress and poverty, and He chose to love them.

d) As seen in His calling of the church

In 1 Corinthians 1:26-29 Paul characterizes the church: "Ye see your calling, brethren, how that not many wise men after the flesh, not many mighty, not many noble, are called; but God hath chosen the foolish things of the world to confound the wise; and God hath chosen the weak things of the world to confound the things which are mighty; and base things of the world, and things which are despised, hath God chosen, yea, and things which are not, to bring to nothing things that are, that no flesh should glory in his presence." The church is made up of common folk. Elsewhere Paul introduces us to some of them: "Know ye not that the unrighteous shall not inherit the kingdom of God? Be not deceived: neither fornicators, nor idolaters, nor adulterers, nor effeminate, nor abusers of themselves with mankind, nor thieves, nor covetous, nor drunkards, nor revilers, nor extortioners, shall inherit the kingdom of God. *And such were some of you*" (1 Cor. 6:9-11, emphasis added). God chose poor, common, sinful people to be part of His church. By His grace He chose them to be rich in spiritual blessings.

3. The riches of the poor

James 2:5 says, "Hath not God chosen the poor of this world to be rich in faith and heirs of the kingdom which he hath promised to them that love him?"

a) The poor are rich in faith

They may never have the riches of the world, but their faith in Christ has brought them eternal riches. All things are theirs in Christ.

(1) Romans 10:12-13—"There is no difference between the Jew and the Greek; for the same Lord over all is rich unto all that call upon him. For whosoever shall call upon the name of the Lord shall be saved." God is rich toward all who come to Him in faith.

(2) Romans 11:33—"Oh, the depth of the riches both of the wisdom and knowledge of God!"

(3) 2 Corinthians 6:10—Paul described himself "as poor, yet making many rich; as having nothing, and yet possessing all things." He had the privilege of making many rich not in a monetary sense but in a spiritual sense.

(4) Philippians 4:19—Paul said, "My God shall supply all your need according to his riches in glory by Christ Jesus."

b) The poor are heirs of the kingdom

What Is the Kingdom?

The kingdom is the sphere of salvation. "Rich in faith" and "heirs of the kingdom" (James 2:5) are two ways of saying the same thing. Calling someone to the kingdom is calling someone to salvation. For example, after Jesus spoke with the ruler who asked, "What good thing shall I do, that I may have eternal life?" (Matt. 19:16), He said, "Verily I say unto you that a rich man shall with difficulty enter into the kingdom of heaven" (v. 23). Jesus equated eternal life with the kingdom of heaven. He went on to say, "It is easier for a camel to go through the eye of a needle, than for a rich man to enter into the kingdom of God" (v. 24). There He equated the kingdom of God with the kingdom of heaven. Then He said to His disciples, "In the regeneration, when the Son of man shall sit on the throne of his glory, ye also shall sit upon twelve thrones, judging the twelve tribes of Israel. And every one that hath forsaken houses, or brethren, or sisters, or father, or mother, or wife, or children, or lands, for my name's sake, shall receive an hundredfold, and shall inherit everlasting life" (vv. 28-29). Therefore, everlasting life, eternal life, the kingdom of God, and the kingdom of heaven are all the same thing.

James 2:5 says that God chose the poor to be "heirs of the kingdom which he hath promised to them that love him." They will inherit the fullness of salvation and the richness of God's eternal blessing. Notice they're described as "them that love him." Faith and love are essential to salvation. When a person puts his faith in Christ and loves Him, he gives evidence of having received the riches of the eternal kingdom of God.

No "Poor Folk" in Heaven

In heaven no one is going to be poor or an outcast. Sometimes I hear preachers say to Christians, "If you mess up your life you're going to have a very small place in heaven." But that's not true. Heaven doesn't have any slums. Everyone's going to be living in the Father's house. We're all going to receive eternal life. We're all going to inherit the promised kingdom in all its glorious fullness. We will all receive the same wages (Matt. 19:30–20:16).

James questioned how his readers could act contrary to the nature of God by looking down on the poor. They were guilty of despising the very people whom God had chosen (v. 6a).

B. The Blasphemy of the Rich (vv. 6b-7)

"Do not rich men oppress you, and draw you before the judgment seats? Do not they blaspheme that worthy name by the which ye are called?" Not only do they drag you before civil courts but also before religious courts. Not only do they depreciate your human value but also your religion. They practice both civil and religious hostility.

91

1. Civil hostility (v. 6)

   "Oppress" means "to tyrannize." Some of the rich were oppressing the poor. The Greek word translated "draw" implies force and pictures dragging someone into court to exploit him by some injustice or inequity.

2. Religious hostility (v. 7)

   The rich were slandering the Lord Jesus Christ. The phrase "by which you are called" speaks of a personal relationship, perhaps referring to their public proclamation of faith at their baptism. From that point on they were known as Christians, meaning, "Christ's own," "Christ's ones," or "belonging to Christ."

Conclusion

James reminded his readers that they belonged to Jesus Christ. They were not to practice partiality by looking down on the poor, whom God has chosen to eternal riches, or by siding with the rich, who oppress the poor and slander the worthy name of Jesus.

Why Christians Must Not Show Partiality

James gives three reasons Christians must not show partiality. First, we are one with the Lord Jesus Christ, who is the glory of God revealed (v. 1). Second, God has chosen the poor to eternal riches (v. 5). And third, God has called us by His name (v. 7). Everything is bound up with the purpose and Person of God in Christ. If we desire to be like Christ—revealing His glory, feeling the way He does, and honoring His name—we cannot be partial. Impartiality must govern our interactions with the poor and the rich.

Focusing on the Facts

1. How does the genealogy of Jesus Christ demonstrate the impartiality of God (see p. 79)?

2. What principle did Jesus teach in the parable of the landowner (Matt. 20:1-16; see pp. 79-80)?

3. In Mark 12:38-44, why did Jesus place a higher value on the widow's offering than He did on the offerings of the rich people (see pp. 80-81)?

4. What did James mean when he said, "Let the brother of low degree rejoice in that he is exalted, but the rich, in that he is made low" (James 1:9-10; see pp. 81-82)?

5. To be partial to the rich and turn your back on the poor is inconsistent in light of the _____ _____ of the poor and the _____ of the rich (James 2:5 7; see p. 82).

6. Who are the poor James refers to in James 2:5 (see p. 82)?

7. Would you agree or disagree with the statement that "rich people have no part in the kingdom of heaven"? Why (see pp. 83-84)?

8. Read Psalm 41:1-3. What special blessings does God promise to those who care for the needs of the poor (see p. 84)?

9. How does meeting the needs of the poor relate to answered prayer (Prov. 21:13; see p. 85)?

10. In what specific ways did God provide for the needs of the poor in the Old Testament (see pp. 86-87)?

11. What does the account of Zacchaeus teach us about the attitude of a saved person toward the poor (Luke 19:1-10; see pp. 87-88)?

12. How does the calling of Israel demonstrate God's mercy toward the poor (Deut. 7:7-8; see p. 89)?

13. What does it mean to be "rich in faith" (James 2:5; see p. 90)?

14. How do you define the kingdom of God (see pp. 90-91)?

15. What is the nature of the civil hostility demonstrated by the rich against the poor (James 2:6-7; see p. 92)?

16. Define the word *Christian* (see p. 92).

17. Why must Christians not show partiality (see p. 92)?

Pondering the Principles

1. Not all believers are poor. In fact, God has blessed many Christians with far more than they need for their daily necessities. Such abundant blessings give opportunity to cultivate good stewardship and generosity. Read 1 Timothy 6:6-19, and answer the following questions. Evaluate both your standard of

living and your standard of giving in light of the principles delineated in that passage.

- Do earthly possessions have any value beyond this life (vv. 6-7)?
- What is God's standard of contentment (v. 8)?
- What pitfalls await those who desire wealth (vv. 9-10)?
- From what is the man of God to flee, and what is he to pursue (vv. 11-12)?
- What attitude is to be avoided by the rich (v. 17)?
- Who is the proper object of our hope and the source of all good things (v. 17)?
- How are the rich to respond to those in need (v. 18)?
- What constitutes true riches (vv. 18-19)?

2. Partiality takes many forms. The prophet Jonah is a classic example of a man who attempted to justify his partiality on spiritual grounds. After all, wasn't Nineveh an exceedingly wicked city (Jonah 1:2)? Why should God show mercy to such a city? And how could God expect Jonah to risk his life preaching to those who had persecuted His people and profaned His name? Read the book of Jonah. How did God convince Jonah of the error of his reasoning (4:1-11)? Is partiality keeping you from reaching out to someone who desperately needs the gracious forgiveness of God? If so, are you willing to set aside your personal feelings for the sake of ministering to that person? Pray that the Lord will give you a heart of compassion toward the lost so that you might experience the joy of being used by Him to minister to their deepest needs.

6
The Evil of Favoritism in the Church—Part 3

Outline

Introduction
A. Favoritism Defined
B. Favoritism Condemned
   1. It is sin
   2. It is contrary to God's nature

Review
  I. The Principle (v. 1)
 II. The Example (vv. 2-4)
III. The Inconsistency (vv. 5-7)
   A. The Divine Choice of the Poor (vv. 5-6a)
   B. The Blasphemy of the Rich (vv. 6b-7)

Lesson
IV. The Violation (vv. 8-11)
   A. Fulfilling the Law (v. 8)
     1. The commendation
     2. The illustration
   B. Transgressing the Law (vv. 9-11)
     1. The sin committed (v. 9)
     2. The standard clarified (vv. 10-11)
       a) Stated (v. 10)
       b) Illustrated (v. 11)
 V. The Appeal (vv. 12-13)
   A. Recognize the Fact of Divine Judgment (v. 12a)
   B. Recognize the Basis for Divine Judgment (vv. 12b-13)
     1. The law
     2. Good works

3. Mercy
   a) The absence of mercy (v. 13*a*)
   b) The triumph of mercy (v. 13*b*)

Conclusion

Introduction

A. Favoritism Defined

"Favoritism" can be defined as a preferential attitude and treatment of a person or group over another having equal claims and rights. It is unjustified partiality. People with equal needs are to be treated with equality. However, we are prone to treat people differently based upon unimportant external considerations such as looks, clothing, possessions, or social standing.

B. Favoritism Condemned

1. It is sin—"If ye have respect of persons, ye commit sin" (James 2:9).

2. It is contrary to God's nature—"The Lord your God is God of gods and Lord of lords, the great God, mighty and awesome, who shows no partiality and accepts no bribes" (Deut. 10:17, NIV). The perfection of God's nature is demonstrated in His impartiality.

Review

I. THE PRINCIPLE (v. 1; see pp. 67-71, 79-81)

II. THE EXAMPLE (vv. 2-4; see pp. 71-75, 81-82

III. THE INCONSISTENCY (vv. 5-7; see pp. 82-92)

A. The Divine Choice of the Poor (vv. 5-6*a*; see pp. 82-91)

B. The Blasphemy of the Rich (vv. 6*b*-7; see pp. 91-92)

Lesson

IV. THE VIOLATION (vv. 8-11)

James has shown that partiality is a violation of God's law because it violates God's attributes, misrepresents the Christian faith, ignores God's choice of the poor, and condones the blasphemous behavior of the rich. Simply put, it is sin.

James also said, "If ye fulfill the royal law according to the scripture, Thou shalt love thy neighbor as thyself, ye do well" (v. 8). Some of his readers were fulfilling the royal law, whereas others were not. Therefore his statements are a combination of commendation (v. 8) and reprimand (vv. 9-11).

A. Fulfilling the Law (v. 8)

"If ye fulfill the royal law according to the scripture, Thou shalt love thy neighbor as thyself, ye do well."

The Royal Law

James 2:8 speaks of "the royal law," or the sovereign law. When a king makes a law, it is supreme and binding. There is no court of appeals at that point. The present tense construction used by James indicates a life-style that is focused upon fulfilling the sovereign law. Jesus taught that the sum of the law is loving "the Lord, thy God, with all thy heart, and with all thy soul, and with all thy mind" and loving "thy neighbor as thyself" (Matt. 22:37-39; cf. Lev. 19:18; Deut. 6:5). True faith is manifest in love for God and for one's neighbor.

When the Bible says to love your neighbor as yourself, it is not referring to the emotional, self-oriented love that is prevalent in our society. Biblical love is always related to meeting needs. To love your neighbor as yourself is to be as concerned with the needs of others as you are with your own needs. When asked, "Who is my neighbor?" Jesus responded by telling about a man who was beaten by robbers and left for dead on a road (Luke 10:30-37). The Good Samaritan cared for him by binding up his wounds and taking him to an inn, where he fed him and left money for his ongoing care.

Jesus was saying that a neighbor is anyone lying in our path with a need. When you come across such a person, take care of him the way you'd take care of yourself. That is the kind of love that fulfills the whole law and is to govern all human relationships.

1. The commendation

If you display such love without partiality, you are fulfilling God's sovereign law and are doing "well" (Gk., *kalōs*). The word *well* means "excellently." You are doing excellently because you are fulfilling God's will by acting in a manner consistent with His nature.

2. The illustration

Hebrews 13:2 tells us that some people who were fulfilling the law of love were actually entertaining angels, although they weren't aware of it. If we judge people on the basis of external criteria, we can easily misjudge them because we don't always know whom we are dealing with. For example, when I was a boy I lived near a golf course. The man who owned the golf course also owned most of the town. Although he was a extremely wealthy man, he dressed like a transient. One day he was walking on the golf course and was picked up by the police and jailed for vagrancy. One of his own employees had turned him in, not knowing who he was. It was not illegal for him to walk on the golf course, but his sloppy appearance led the employee to assume that he was out of place. He didn't fit the country-club image. Indeed, we don't always know with whom we are dealing.

To fulfill the royal law is to love others as we love ourselves —and to do so without partiality.

B. Transgressing the Law (vv. 9-11)

1. The sin committed (v. 9)

"But if ye have respect of persons, ye commit sin, and are convicted of the law as transgressors."

Within the congregation to whom James wrote were some who were violating the royal law by being partial. As a result they were convicted by the law as sinners and transgressors (Deut. 1:17; 16:19).

Two words in verse 9 refer to sin: "Sin" (Gk., *hamartia*, "to come short of the mark") and "transgressors" (Gk., *parabatēs*, "one who goes beyond the limits"). One says you've fallen too short, the other says you've gone too far. Sin is either coming short of God's perfect standard or going beyond His law.

To identify someone as a transgressor of the law is to characterize him as a lawbreaker. James doesn't say, "You have transgressed the law"; he says, "You are a transgressor." If you show partiality, you characterize yourself as a violator of God's law.

2. The standard clarified (vv. 10-11)

a) Stated (v. 10)

"Whosoever shall keep the whole law, and yet offend in one point, he is guilty of all."

Violation of one point of the law makes you a transgressor of the whole law.

The Unity of God's Law

We have an obligation to obey all God's law. To break the law at even one point is to be characterized as a sinner and a transgressor who willfully defies God's authority. Jesus said, "Whosoever . . . shall break one of these least commandments, and shall teach men so, he shall be called the least in the kingdom of heaven" (Matt. 5:19). William Barclay said, "The Jew was very apt to regard the law as a series of detached injunctions. To keep one was to gain credit; to break one was to incur debt. A man could add up the ones he kept and subtract the ones he broke and so emerge with a credit or a debit balance. There was a rabbinic saying, 'Whoever fulfills only one law, good is appointed to him; his days are prolonged and he will inherit the land' " (*The Letters of James and Peter* [Philadelphia: Westminster, 1976], p. 69).

The rabbis weren't the only ones deceived by such thinking. Many people today are under the illusion that there is some kind of divine credit/debit balance being kept. If the laws they don't break outnumber the laws they do break, they assume everything will be OK. However, the unity of God's law dictates that when we violate one point of the law we violate the entire law. We cannot justify our sin by saying, "I committed only little sins like prejudice, partiality, and indifference to the poor; I certainly didn't commit the big sins like murder and adultery!" Although it is true that not all sins are equally heinous or damaging, they all shatter the unity of God's law and turn us into violators, rebels, and transgressors.

The law of God is the transcript of the divine mind—it reflects His character and will. The essential thing that God desires regarding His law is an attitude of submission. Any violation of the law strikes a blow at God by demonstrating a refusal to love Him and submit to His authority. The true believer desires to keep God's law. When he breaks it he sees himself as a transgressor and comes to the Savior for cleansing and forgiveness. The Lawgiver is one, and the law is one. One sin violates the entire law because it violates the character and will of the Lawgiver.

b) Illustrated (v. 11)

> "He that said, Do not commit adultery, said also, Do not kill. Now if thou commit no adultery, yet if thou kill, thou art become a transgressor of the law."

James chose for his illustrations the two most severe social sins, both of which carried the death penalty in the Old Testament. He personalized the illustrations by using the personal pronoun "thou" ("you"). If you commit murder but do not commit adultery, you have still transgressed the whole law.

The sins of murder and adultery may seem far removed from the sin of favoritism. However, I believe James put favoritism in such serious company to illustrate that it can lead to hate, which is the attitude behind murder.

Partiality is a serious sin because it violates the sovereign law of God by withholding love for one's neighbor. Those who practice partiality are condemned as transgressors of the entire law.

V. THE APPEAL (vv. 12-13)

A. Recognize the Fact of Divine Judgment (v. 12a)

"So speak ye, and so do, as they that shall be judged."

James was telling his readers to speak and act as people who are headed for future judgment.

B. Recognize the Basis for Divine Judgment (vv. 12b-13)

"By the law of liberty. For he shall have judgment without mercy, that hath shown no mercy; and mercy rejoiceth against judgment."

1. The law

The "law of liberty" is the totality of God's law or His Word, the Scripture. It is a law of liberty because it, frees us from slavery to sin and brings us to eternal freedom and glory. It frees us from the curse of death and hell. It is the truth (John 17:17), so it frees us from the search for truth. And it calls us to serve God freely out of love rather than by outward restraint. The Word of God is in every sense a law of freedom and liberation.

2. Good works

With regard to judgment Paul said, "God . . . will render to every man according to his deeds: to them who by patient continuance in well-doing seek for glory and honor and immortality, eternal life; but unto them that are contentious, and do not obey the truth, but obey unrighteousness, indignation and wrath . . . but glory, honor, and peace, to every man that worketh good. . . . For there is no respect of persons with God" (Rom. 2:5-11). God will not be partial in judgment. Everyone will be judged on the basis of his works.

That truth is not contradictory to the fact that we will be saved on the basis of our faith in Christ. True faith is manifest through righteous deeds. Ephesians 2:10 says, "We are his workmanship, created in Christ Jesus unto good works, which God hath before ordained that we should walk in them." A life in which God is producing good works gives evidence of true salvation. Redemption always brings about obedient living. The nature of the New Covenant is God's writing of His law upon our hearts (Jer. 31:31-34). The result is the freedom to love and obey God from the heart. Obviously we have our times of disobedience, but the overall pattern of the redeemed is a fruitful, obedient life.

3. Mercy

    a) The absence of mercy (v. 13*a*)

        "He shall have judgment without mercy, that hath shown no mercy."

        The person who shows no mercy or compassion —who shows favoritism, partiality, and disregard for people with needs—will have no mercy in judgment. That's because he's obviously not a redeemed person.

Judgment Without Mercy

The phrase "judgment without mercy" must mean eternal hell—strict, full, unrelieved judgment, every sin receiving its just punishment to the fullest. The gospel transforms the heart, making us like God, who is merciful, compassionate, and impartial. True believers will demonstrate those godly characteristics. If your life is not characterized by deeds of mercy, it is evident that the life of God is not in you. Jesus said, "Blessed are the merciful; for they shall obtain mercy" (Matt. 5:7). Where mercy is given, mercy is received.

James describes no specific moment of judgment, but the allusion is to the judgment that comes when the Lord Jesus returns as Judge.

b) The triumph of mercy (v. 13*b*)

"Mercy rejoiceth against judgment."

That's to say mercy triumphs over judgment. If your life is characterized by mercy, you will escape judgment because you have a transformed life. Bible scholar James Rosscup wrote, "When a man lives without mercy to others in God's world, he simply shows off the fact that he himself has never responded aright to the immeasurable mercy of God. . . . The mercy a man has shown others as fruit of a life touched by God's saving mercy will triumph over judgment. His own sins, worthy of judgment, are removed by God's working in his life [dissolving] all the charges strict justice might bring against him. Thus his showing of mercy is not a matter of heaping up personal merit to deserve salvation by his own good works. The mercy he shows is itself a work of God for which he can take no credit" (*General Epistles —Syllabus on James* [Rosscup, 1977], pp. 19-20].

If it is characteristic of you to demonstrate mercy without partiality, meeting people at the point of their need no matter who they are, you give evidence of having received such mercy and of being transformed by the power of God. You are therefore ready for the Judgment Day.

Conclusion

James has shown that partiality is inconsistent with the Christian faith because of the impartial nature of God, the purpose and plan of God in choosing the poor of this world to be rich in spiritual blessings, and the command to love your neighbor as yourself. In addition, partiality violates the entire law of God and makes a person a transgressor in danger of eternal judgment. If you come before the judgment of God without having manifested mercy in your life, He will show you no mercy because you have not shown evidence of true salvation. On the other hand, if He looks at your life and sees a pattern of mercy toward others and impartiality toward those in need, you will triumph over judgment.

James calls us to examine our lives. Is your life characterized by impartiality? Are you gracious, kind, thoughtful, and loving toward those in need? Do you seek to provide for their needs without favoritism? When you fail to show impartiality, do you confess your sin and seek forgiveness and restoration? Those are the marks of true, saving faith. The absence of such is reason for grave concern and should prompt a deeper examination of your heart to see if your faith is real.

Focusing on the Facts

1. Define favoritism (see p. 96).
2. Why is favoritism a violation of God's law (see p. 97)?
3. What is the "royal law" (v. 8; see pp. 97-98)?
4. In what way does fulfilling the royal law eliminate partiality (see p. 97)?
5. Biblical love is always related to _____ _____ (see p. 97).
6. What was our Lord's response when asked, "Who is my neighbor?" (Luke 10:30-37; see p. 97)?
7. What is the difference in meaning between "sin" and "transgressor" in verse 9 (see p. 99)?
8. What did some of the rabbis teach about keeping the law? Why were they wrong (see pp. 99-100)?
9. What does our breaking of the law reveal about our attitude toward God (see p. 100)?
10. In what sense is the law a "law of liberty" (v. 12; see p. 101)?
11. How do good works relate to future judgment (Rom. 2:5-11; Eph. 2:8-10; see pp. 101-2)?
12. What will be the role of mercy in future judgment (v. 13; see pp. 102-3)?
13. List the ways in which partiality is inconsistent with the Christian faith (see p. 103).

Pondering the Principles

1. To love one's neighbor as oneself is to fulfill the royal law (James 2:8). In recent years there has been much discussion about the need to have a healthy self-love or self-esteem before we can properly love others. But is that the biblical perspective? When

Jesus instructed us to love our neighbors as ourselves (Matt. 22:37-39), He did not teach love of self; He knew self-love already existed. His emphasis was to redirect our love from self to others. Review the section entitled "The Royal Law" (see pp. 97-98). What does it mean to love one's neighbor? Read the following verses, noting the characteristics of godly love, and pray for the Lord to help you set aside self-love for the sake of loving others: John 3:16; 15:12-13; Romans 5:5-10; Galatians 5:22-23; Ephesians 5:25-29; Philippians 1:9-11; 1 John 2:5; 4:12; 5:1-3.

2. The tender mercy of God is a recurring theme throughout Scripture. Those who have experienced His gracious salvation received an incomparable degree of mercy. Therefore, Christians should be the most merciful people of all. Does mercy characterize your life? If you have lost your perspective on how merciful God has been to you, spend time in prayer, reflecting upon His goodness and loving-kindness. Read the prayers of Mary and Zacharias as they recited His mercy toward His people throughout history (Luke 1:46-55, 68-79). Be diligent in praising the Lord for the depth of His great mercy, and be sure to show mercy to those around you.

7
Dead Faith

Outline

Introduction
A. Unrighteous Faith
   1. Matthew 5:16
   2. John 8:31-32
B. Righteous Faith

Lesson
I. The Character of Dead Faith (vv. 14-20)
   A. Empty Confession (v. 14)
      1. John 15:2, 6
      2. James 2:13
      3. Romans 2:6-10
   B. False Compassion (vv. 15-17)
      1. The problem defined (v. 15)
      2. The provision denied (v. 16)
      3. The peril described (v. 17)
   C. Shallow Conviction (vv. 18-20)
      1. The challenge (v. 18)
      2. The commendation (v. 19*a*)
      3. The condemnation (vv. 19*b*-20)
         a) Demonic faith (v. 19*b*)
         b) Dead faith (v. 20)
Conclusion

Introduction

According to James, faith that doesn't result in obedience is dead: "What doth it profit, my brethren, though a man say he hath faith, and have not works? Can that faith save him? If a brother or sister be naked, and destitute of daily food, and one of you say unto them, Depart in peace, be ye warmed and filled; notwithstanding, ye give them not those things which are needful to the body, what doth it profit? Even so faith, if it hath not works, is dead, being alone. Yea, a man may say, Thou hast faith, and I have works; show me thy faith without thy works, and I will show thee my faith by my works. Thou believest that there is one God; thou doest well. The demons also believe, and tremble. But wilt thou know, O vain man, that faith without works is dead?" (James 2:14-20).

A. Unrighteous Faith

The New Testament speaks of a faith that does not save. That kind of faith is marked by a failure to produce righteous deeds.

1. Matthew 5:16—Jesus said to His disciples, "Let your light so shine before men, that they may see your good works, and glorify your Father, who is in heaven." The light that shines from a believer's life is the light of good works. Jesus went on to say, "Not every one that saith unto me, Lord, Lord, shall enter into the kingdom of heaven, but he that doeth the will of my Father" (7:21). The hallmark of saving faith is obedience to the will of God, not empty words.

2. John 8:31-32—Jesus said to a group of Jewish followers, "If ye continue in my word, then are ye my disciples indeed; and ye shall know the truth, and the truth shall make you free." Their initial belief was exposed as non-saving faith when they rejected His words and sought to kill Him (cf. vv. 40-45).

Caution: Knowledge Does Not Equal Saving Faith

To equate a simple knowledge of the gospel facts with saving faith is deception. People who believe the facts of the gospel but make no irrevocable commitment to shun sin and serve the Lord Jesus possess a dead, fruitless faith. They need to be confronted with the reality of their separation from God (cf. Isa. 59:2). James did not permit any such deception to go unchallenged. His epistle repeatedly calls us to examine our faith in light of our works.

B. Righteous Faith

In saying that a redeemed life will manifest righteous works, James is not teaching salvation by works. The clear teaching of Scripture is that salvation is by grace through faith, "not of works, lest any man should boast" (Eph. 2:9). The issue is not salvation by works, but a salvation that produces works.

Some of the Jews to whom James wrote were genuine believers; some were not. Nevertheless, all had outwardly identified with the Christian faith. Legalistic Judaism had imposed upon the people impossible standards of behavior. That's why Jesus described the scribes and Pharisees as those who "bind heavy burdens and grievous to be borne, and lay them on men's shoulders" (Matt. 23:4). In contrast, the gospel of Jesus Christ brought grace, freedom, joy, and the power to produce truly righteous works.

It's possible that some Jewish believers misunderstood the nature of Christian freedom and went from the extreme of legalism to the other extreme. Perhaps they reasoned that since good works cannot produce salvation, they are unnecessary altogether. Some may have affirmed their belief in the gospel apart from a response of obedience. Regardless of the specific situation, some were content to be self-deceived hearers of the Word rather than obedient doers (James 1:22).

Lesson

James gives us three characteristics of dead faith: empty confession (v. 14), false compassion (vv. 15-17), and shallow conviction (vv. 18-20).

I. THE CHARACTER OF DEAD FAITH (vv. 14-20)

A. Empty Confession (v. 14)

"What doth it profit, my brethren, though a man say he hath faith, and have not works? Can [that] faith save him?"

James used the present tense to indicate that even though a person may continue to profess faith in God, his claim is useless if he doesn't obey Him. That principle is consistent throughout the New Testament.

1. John 15:2, 6—Jesus said, "Every branch in me that beareth not fruit [the Father] taketh away. . . . If a man abide not in me, he is cast forth as a branch and is withered; and men gather them, and cast them into the fire, and they are burned." The fruitless branch represents someone who outwardly identifies with Christ but does not possess spiritual life. Therefore he does not produce spiritual fruit.

2. James 2:13—James said that God will be merciless to those who show no mercy because an absence of mercy demonstrates an absence of saving faith. A transformed life will produce behavior consistent with its new nature.

3. Romans 2:6-10—Paul said that God will judge a person "according to his deeds: to them who by patient continuance in well-doing seek for glory and honor and immortality, eternal life; but unto them that are contentious, and do not obey the truth, but obey unrighteousness, indignation and wrath, tribulation and anguish, upon every soul of man that doeth evil. . . . But glory, honor, and peace, to every man that worketh good." We will be judged on the basis of our deeds because our deeds reveal who we really are.

James Versus Paul?

Some people believe there is conflict between James' teaching on works and Paul's teaching on grace.

1. Paul on grace

   a) Romans 11:6—"If [election] is by grace, it is no longer on the basis of works, otherwise grace is no longer grace" (NASB).

b) Galatians 2:16—"A man is not justified by the works of the law, but by the faith of Jesus Christ, even we have believed in Jesus Christ, that we might be justified by the faith of Christ, and not by the works of the law; for by the works of the law shall no flesh be justified."

c) Ephesians 2:8-10—"By grace are ye saved through faith; and that not of yourselves, it is the gift of God not of works, lest any man should boast. For we are his workmanship, created in Christ Jesus unto good works, which God hath before ordained that we should walk in them."

2. James on grace

James affirmed salvation by sovereign grace when he wrote, "Of his own will begot he us with the word of truth, that we should be a kind of first fruits of his creatures" (James 1:18). God saved us by His own will through the word of truth so He might make us new creatures. Both James and Paul taught that sovereign redemption is manifested in good works.

3. Paul on works

a) 2 Timothy 2:19—"Let every one that nameth the name of Christ depart from iniquity."

b) Titus 1:16—Regarding false teachers on the isle of Crete, Paul said, "They profess that they know God, but in works they deny him, being abominable, and disobedient, and unto every good work reprobate." The Greek word translated "reprobate" refers to a confused, disoriented, and wicked mind. They profess to know God, but their evil works reveal the true condition of their hearts.

c) Titus 2:7—Paul exhorted Titus, saying, "In all things [show] thyself a pattern of good works." Although Paul affirmed the sovereignty of God in salvation, he also affirmed that true salvation results in submission to the authority of Christ, an abandonment of sin, and a pattern of good works. All spiritual leaders are to exemplify such a life-style.

d) Acts 19:18-19—After Paul preached the gospel in Ephesus, many of the new converts, who had been involved in magic and the occult, gave public testimony of their allegiance to Christ by burning their magic books.

e) 1 Thessalonians 1:9—Paul commended the Thessalonian believers because they "turned to God from idols, to serve the living and true God." Salvation involves serving a new master.

A new Christian will not fully understand all the implications of turning from sin to serve Christ; that's an ever-increasing awareness, even in the life of a mature believer. But each believer is a new creation in whom the Holy Spirit is producing Christlike characteristics and behavior.

Paul and James were not at odds with each other. Each emphasized a different aspect of true salvation. Paul addressed the heresy of salvation *by* works and concluded that man cannot *become* a Christian by his own efforts. He is saved by grace. James addressed the heresy of salvation *without* works and concluded that a man cannot *be* a Christian if his behavior does not reflect a transformed heart. He is saved for works.

In 2 Corinthians 13:5 Paul says, "Examine yourselves, whether you are in the faith." Look carefully at the product of your life. What you see reveals what you are. An empty confession is evidence of a dead faith.

B. False Compassion (vv. 15-17)

1. The problem defined (v. 15)

"If a brother or sister be naked, and destitute of daily food."

False compassion is marked by an absence of good deeds. In context the brother or sister isn't stark naked, but without adequate clothing. The Greek word translated "destitute" here means "deprived of daily food" or "starving to death." True believers will respond by meeting that need (cf. 1 John 3:17-18).

2. The provision denied (v. 16)

"One of you say unto them, Depart in peace, be ye warmed and filled; notwithstanding, ye give them not those things which are needful to the body, what doth it profit?"

"Depart in peace" was a common Jewish expression. It was similar to "God bless you." But what good are pious words if pressing needs are neglected?

3. The peril described (v. 17)

"Even so faith, if it hath not works, is dead, being alone."

In Matthew 25 Jesus speaks of coming judgment: "When the Son of man shall come in his glory, and all the holy angels with him, then shall he sit upon the throne of his glory. And before him shall be gathered all the nations; and he shall separate them one from another, as a shepherd divideth his sheep from the goats. And he shall set the sheep on his right hand, but the goats on the left.

"Then shall the King say unto them on his right hand, Come, ye blessed of my Father, inherit the kingdom prepared for you from the foundation of the world; for I was hungry, and ye gave me food; I was thirsty, and ye gave me drink; I was a stranger, and ye took me in; naked, and ye clothed me; I was sick, and ye visited me; I was in prison, and ye came unto me. Then shall the righteous answer him, saying, Lord, when saw we thee hungry, and fed thee; or thirsty, and gave thee drink: When saw we thee a stranger, and took thee in; or naked, and clothed thee? Or when saw we thee sick, or in prison, and came unto thee? And the King shall answer and say unto them, Verily I say unto you, Inasmuch as ye have done it unto one of the least of these my brethren, ye have done it unto me. Then shall he say also unto them on the left hand, Depart from me, ye cursed, into everlasting fire, prepared for the devil and his angels. . . . And these shall go away into everlasting punishment, but the righteous into life eternal" (vv. 31-41, 46).

The sheep, whose true faith is demonstrated by their compassion, will enter the kingdom. The goats, whose lack of saving faith is revealed by their lack of compassion, will be shut out.

C. Shallow Conviction (vv. 18-20)

1. The challenge (v. 18)

"Yea, a man may say, Thou hast faith, and I have works; show me thy faith without thy works, and I will show thee my faith by my works."

James was probably referring to himself as the one possessing true faith. Speaking in the third person is consistent with his emphasis on humility (cf. James 4:10).

His challenge is formidable: show faith without works. The Greek word translated "show" means "to exhibit," "to demonstrate," or "to put on display." The point is it can't be done. The only way to demonstrate true faith is through righteous deeds.

Resources and Responsibilities

The standard for Christian obedience is extremely high, but it is also important to note that our resources in Christ are inexhaustible.

1. The believer's resources

   a) We are called to glory and virtue (2 Pet. 1:3).

   b) We are partakers of the divine nature (2 Pet. 1:4).

   c) We have escaped worldly corruption (2 Pet. 1:4).

   d) We have overcome Satan's evil world system (1 John 5:4-5).

   e) We have overcome the evil one himself (1 John 2:13-14).

2. The believer's responsibilities

Christians must be diligent to cultivate the godly characteristics that are part of their new nature. Peter said, "Giving all diligence, add to your faith, virtue; and to virtue, knowledge; and to knowledge, self-control; and to self-control, patience; and to patience, godliness; and to godliness, brotherly kindness; and to brotherly kindness, love. For if these things be in you, and abound, they make you that ye shall neither be barren nor unfruitful in the knowledge of our Lord Jesus Christ. But he that lacketh these things is blind and cannot see afar off, and hath forgotten that he was purged from his old sins" (2 Pet. 1:5-9).

If those virtues are increasing in your life, you will have the joy and assurance that you are a productive child of God. If they are lacking, you will lose not only the joy of serving God but also might even doubt your salvation.

2. The commendation (v. 19*a*)

"Thou believest that there is one God; thou doest well."

The Hebrew *Shema* is a classic statement of the Jewish faith: "The Lord our God is one Lord" (Deut. 6:4). Because the Jewish people prided themselves on their orthodoxy, it is not surprising that the response to James's challenge came by way of a doctrinal statement. James's "thou doest well" is intentionally sarcastic.

3. The condemnation (vv. 19*b*-20)

a) Demonic faith (v. 19*b*)

"The demons also believe, and tremble."

Affirmation of orthodox doctrine is not necessarily proof of saving faith. Demons affirm the oneness of God and tremble at its implications, but they are not redeemed. Some demons said to Jesus, "What have we to do with thee, Jesus, thou Son of God? Art thou come here to torment us before the time?" (Matt. 8:29). They knew that Jesus was the Son of God and that He would judge them.

James implies that demonic faith is greater than dead faith: demonic faith produces fear, whereas unbelieving men have "no fear of God before their eyes" (Rom. 3:18).

Exposing Shallow Conviction

The Puritan writer Thomas Manton described nonsaving faith in graphic terms. He said it is "a simple and naked assent to such things as are propounded in the word of God, and maketh men more knowing but not better, not more holy or heavenly. They that have it may believe the promises, the doctrines, the precepts as well as the histories . . . but yet, lively saving faith it is not, for he who hath that, findeth his heart engaged to Christ, and doth so believe the promises of the gospel concerning pardon of sins and life eternal that he seeketh after them as his happiness, and doth so believe the mysteries of our redemption by Christ as that all his hope and peace and confidence is drawn from thence, and doth so believe the threatenings, whether of temporal plagues or eternal damnation, as that, in comparison of them, all the frightful things of the world are as nothing" (*The Complete Works of Thomas Manton*, vol. 17 [London: James Nisbet, 1874], pp. 113-14).

Manton went on to describe shallow conviction as nothing more than "temporary faith, which is an assent to scriptural or gospel truth, accompanied with a slight and insufficient touch upon the heart, called 'a taste of the heavenly gift, and of the good word of God, and the powers of the world to come,' Heb. vi. 4-6. By this kind of faith, the mind is not only enlightened, but the heart affected with some joy, and the life in some measure reformed, at least from grosser sins, called, '[escaping] the pollutions of the world' (2 Peter ii.20; but the impression is not deep enough, nor is the joy and delight rooted enough to encounter all temptations to the contrary. Therefore, this sense of religion may be choked, or worn off, either by the cares of this world, or by voluptuous living, or by great and bitter persecutions and troubles for righteousness' sake.

"It is a common deceit: many are persuaded that Jesus is the Christ, the only Son of God, and so are moved to embrace his person, and in some measure to obey his precepts, and to depend upon his promises, and fear his threatenings, and so by consequence to have their hearts loosened from the world in part, and seem to prefer Christ and their duty to him above worldly things,

116

as long as no temptations do assault their resolutions, or sensual objects stand not up in any considerable strength to entice them; but at length, when they find his laws so strict and spiritual, and contrary either to the bent of their affections or worldly interests, they fall off, and lose all their taste and relish of the hopes of the gospel, and so declare plainly that they were not rooted and grounded in the faith and hope thereof" (p. 114).

b) Dead faith (v. 20)

"But wilt thou know, O vain man, that faith without works is dead?"

The word translated "dead" (Gk., *argē*) means "to be fruitless." He who has faith without works is as destitute as a dead tree.

A Scriptural Illustration of Dead Faith

In Acts 8 Luke records the ministry of Philip at Samaria: "The people with one accord gave heed unto those things which Philip spoke, hearing and seeing the miracles which he did. . . . But there was a certain man, called Simon, who previously . . . used sorcery, and bewitched the people of Samaria, giving out that himself was some great one, to whom they all gave heed, from the least to the greatest, saying, This man is the great power of God. And to him they had regard, because that for a long time he had bewitched them with sorceries. But when they believed Philip preaching the things concerning the kingdom of God, and the name of Jesus Christ, they were baptized, both men and women. . . .

"Then Simon himself believed also; and when he was baptized, he continued with Philip, and was amazed, beholding the miracles and signs which were done. . . . [Peter and John] prayed for [the Samaritan believers] that they might receive the Holy Spirit; for as yet he was fallen upon none of them. . . . Then laid they their hands on them, and they received the Holy Spirit. And when Simon saw that through laying on of the apostles' hands the Holy Spirit was given, he offered them money, saying, Give me also this power, that on whomsoever I lay hands, he may receive the Holy Spirit.

"But Peter said unto him, Thy money perish with thee, because thou hast thought that the gift of God may be purchased with money. Thou hast neither part nor lot in this matter; for thy heart is not right in the sight of God. Repent, therefore, of this thy wickedness, and pray God, if perhaps the thought of thine heart may be forgiven thee; for I perceive that thou art in the gall of bitterness, and in the bond of iniquity" (vv. 6-23).

Simon believed, was baptized, was amazed at the power of the Holy Spirit, and continued with Philip, yet was in danger of perishing (v. 20) because his heart was not right with God (v. 21). In reality he was enslaved to sin (v. 23). His only hope was to repent and seek God's forgiveness (v. 22).

Conclusion

Simon illustrates a frightening reality: It is possible to go through the motions of Christianity and still be eternally lost. Such is the nature of dead faith. According to James, true faith will be evidenced by righteous deeds, not by empty claims.

Focusing on the Facts

1. What label does James give to faith that doesn't produce the fruit of obedience (v. 17; see p. 107-8)?
2. According to Jesus, what is the proof of a true disciple (John 8:31; see p. 108)?
3. What are the three characteristics of dead faith according to James (James 2:14-20; see p. 109)?
4. Is it possible to profess belief in the gospel and still be unsaved? Explain (see pp. 109-10).
5. The fruitless branch in John 15:2 refers to whom (see p. 110)?
6. Why will those who show no mercy receive no mercy from God (James 2:13; see p. 110)?
7. How do we resolve the apparent conflict between James and Paul on the issue of faith and works (see pp. 110-12)?
8. In Matthew 25:31-46, what distinguishes a sheep from a goat (see pp. 113-14)?
9. What is the challenge presented in James 2:18? Is it possible to respond to that challenge? Explain (see p. 114).

10. What are the resources and responsibilities of the believer (see pp. 114-15)?
11. Why is an affirmation of orthodox doctrine inadequate proof of saving faith (see pp. 115-16)?
12. Some Bible students believe that Simon the sorcerer was a true believer. Do you agree or disagree? Explain (Acts 8:4-25; see pp. 117-18).

Pondering the Principles

1. We have seen the tragic reality of a faith that does not save. Throughout His earthly ministry Jesus repeatedly confronted such faith. On one occasion Jesus addressed Jewish followers who had believed in Him, describing the relationship between doctrine and deed (John 8:12-47). Read that passage carefully, and make a list of doctrines and deeds that characterize dead faith, as well as a corresponding list of those that characterize true faith. What did Jesus conclude about the quality of their belief? What would He conclude about yours? Do your deeds reflect the truth of your doctrine?

2. Do you know that God will never ask a believer to do something He hasn't already empowered him to do? For example, Paul's admonition to the Philippian believers to "work out [their] own salvation with fear and trembling" (Phil. 2:12) was based upon the reality that it was "God who worketh in [them] both to will and to do of his good pleasure" (Phil. 2:13). God had supplied the divine resources; their responsibility was to mature in their Christian life. Review the section entitled "Resources and Responsibilities" (see pp. 114-15). Spend time in prayer thanking God for His gracious provisions and seeking His wisdom and strength in the daily application of your divine resources.

3. Review Thomas Manton's insightful descriptions of nonsaving faith and shallow conviction (see pp. 116-17). Is your heart "engaged to Christ"? Do you find joy, hope, peace, and confidence in the reality of your redemption? Perhaps you felt concern as you identified with his description of shallow conviction. Ask the Lord to reveal any instance where you're holding to an affirmation of faith without corresponding obedience. Be faithful to expose your life to the probing light of God's Word.

8
Living Faith

Outline

Introduction

Review
I. The Character of Dead Faith (vv. 14-20)
    A. Empty Confession (v. 14)
    B. False Compassion (vv. 15-17)
    C. Shallow Conviction (vv. 18-20)

Lesson
II. The Contrast of Living Faith (vv. 21-26)
    A. Abraham (vv. 21-24)
       1. Abraham's seed (v. 21*a*)
       2. Abraham's salvation (vv. 21*b*-24)
          a) The means of salvation: faith (Rom. 4:1-25)
             (1) Justified by faith, not works (vv. 1-8)
             (2) Justified by grace, not law (vv. 9-17)
             (3) Justified by divine power, not human effort (vv. 18-25)
          b) The manifestation of salvation: works (James 2:21*b*-24)
             (1) The testing of his faith (v. 21*b*)
             (2) The perfection of his faith (v. 22)
             (3) The results of his faith (v. 23)
             (4) The vindication of his faith (v. 24)
    B. Rahab (v. 25)
       1. Her situation
       2. Her salvation
    C. A Corpse (v. 26)

Conclusion

Introduction

Scripture teaches the frightening reality of a faith that doesn't save a person from hell. It's possible to believe all the gospel facts yet remain unsaved. James called such a faith dead faith (James 2:20) and exhorted his readers to be "doers of the word and not hearers only" (1:22). He wanted them to understand that a true believer is not content simply to hear the Word of God, but rather, he obeys it. True faith results in a changed life.

Although faith is invisible, the presence of true faith is evidenced by a changed life. It's not enough to say you have faith; that proves nothing. If your life doesn't demonstrate righteous deeds, you have no spiritual life within you. After all, we've been *created in Christ Jesus unto good works*, which God hath before ordained that we should walk in them" (Eph. 2:10, emphasis added). The absence of good works indicates the absence of saving faith.

Jesus said, "Many will say to me . . . Lord, Lord, have we not prophesied in thy name? And in thy name have cast out demons? And in thy name done many wonderful works? And then will I profess unto them, I never knew you; depart from me, ye that work iniquity" (Matt. 7:22-23). Those people called Him "Lord" but did not obey Him (v. 21). The pattern of their lives invalidated their claim to salvation.

Review

I. THE CHARACTER OF DEAD FAITH (vv. 14-20; see pp. 109-18)

   A. Empty Confession (v. 14; see pp. 109-12)

   B. False Compassion (vv. 15-17; see pp. 112-14)

   C. Shallow Conviction (vv. 18-20; see pp. 114-18)

Lesson

II. THE CONTRAST OF LIVING FAITH (vv. 21-26)

In contrast to the three characteristics of dead faith, James gives us three illustrations of living faith.

A. Abraham (vv. 21-24)

"Was not Abraham, our father, justified by works, when he had offered Isaac, his son, upon the altar? Seest thou how faith wrought with his works, and by works was faith made perfect? And the scripture was fulfilled which saith, Abraham believed God, and it was imputed unto him for righteousness; and he was called the friend of God. Ye see, then, that by works a man is justified, and not by faith only."

1. Abraham's seed (v. 21a)

James may have used the phrase "our father" in a racial sense, since Abraham is the progenitor of the Jewish people (cf. John 8:37; Rom. 4:1; James 1:1). But the fatherhood of Abraham is more than racial. In a sense he is the father of all who believe in God, whether Jew or Gentile. Paul told the Galatians, "They who are of faith . . . are the sons of Abraham. . . . They who are of faith are blessed with faithful Abraham" (Gal. 3:7, 9). Abraham is the classic biblical illustration of saving faith.

2. Abraham's salvation (vv. 21b-24)

a) The means of salvation: faith (Rom. 4:1-25)

The Greek word translated "justified" means "to be considered right with God." In Romans 4 Paul delineates three characteristics of Abraham's justification.

(1) Justified by faith, not works (vv. 1-8)

Chapter 4 begins, "What shall we say, then, that Abraham, our father, as pertaining to the flesh, hath found? For if Abraham were justified by works, he hath something of which to glory, but not before God. For what saith the scripture? Abraham believed God, and it was counted unto him for righteousness. Now to him that worketh is the reward not reckoned of grace, but of debt. But to him that worketh not, but believeth on him that justifieth the ungodly, his faith is counted for righteousness. Even as David also describeth the blessedness of the man unto whom God imputeth righteousness apart from works, saying, Blessed are they whose iniquities are forgiven, and whose sins are covered. Blessed is the man to whom the Lord will not impute sin" (vv. 1-8). Abraham was justified by faith, not by works.

(2) Justified by grace, not law (vv. 9-17)

Verse 16 tells us that the promise to Abraham "is of faith, that it might be by grace."

(3) Justified by divine power, not human effort (vv. 18-25)

Abraham was "fully persuaded that, what [God] had promised, he was able also to perform. And therefore it was imputed to him for righteousness" (vv. 21-22). In the same way, righteousness will be imputed to all who "believe on him who raised up Jesus, our Lord, from the dead" (v. 24).

Paul said to the Galatians: "Abraham believed God, and it was accounted to him for righteousness. Know ye, therefore, that they who are of faith, the same are the sons of Abraham. . . . No man is justified by the law in the sight of God, it is evident; for, The just shall live by faith" (3:6-7, 11).

Abraham was justified by grace, which is God's un-merited favor. Paul said, "If Abraham were justified by works, he hath something of which to glory, *but not before God*" (Rom. 4:2, emphasis added). A man cannot be justified by works "before God." God knew Abraham was like all sinners, spiritually and morally bankrupt. On the basis of Abraham's faith, however, God granted him an imputed righteousness. The Greek word translated "imputed" means "to deposit to one's account." God deposits to the repentant sinner's bankrupt account the righteousness necessary for dwelling in the presence of God.

Abraham received God's imputed righteousness when "he believed in the Lord [so God] counted it to him for righteousness" (Gen. 15:6). God clothed him with righteousness (cf. Isa. 61:10). So it is with all who trust God. When you put your faith in Jesus Christ, righteousness is imputed to you. It's not something you are born with or earn; you receive it as a gift from God. That's the marvel of salvation by grace through faith.

Faith: The Sole Condition of Salvation

Believing God has always been the sole condition of salvation. How much does a person have to believe about God to be saved? As much as He has revealed about Himself. You are responsible to believe whatever God has revealed to you thus far.

Abraham didn't have the benefit of the Old and New Testaments and knew little about God. When he was about seventy-five years old and living in Ur of the Chaldeans God said to him, "Get thee out of thy country, and from thy kindred, and from thy father's house, unto a land that I will show thee" (Gen. 12:1). Abraham did just that. He believed what God said and was thereby justified.

There is no salvation by works. Paul said, "By the deeds of the law there shall no flesh be justified in [God's] sight. . . . Being justified freely by his grace" (Romans 3:20, 24). We are saved when we respond in faith to the sovereign grace that God dispenses to us.

Although James affirmed that "Abraham believed God, and it was imputed unto him for righteousness" (James 2:23), he also said Abraham was "justified by works" (James 2:21). There is no contradiction. Abraham was justified by faith in the sight of God and by works in the sight of men.

Why Did God Forgive Abraham?

Faith in God brings forgiveness through Christ. Christ's sacrificial death on the cross was the basis for Abraham's forgiveness. He was forgiven because Christ would in the future pay the penalty for his sins, just as Christ's death paid the penalty for every believer —past, present, and future.

b) The manifestation of salvation: works (James 2:21*b*-24)

Works are the only way faith can be verified as genuine saving faith. That is the key element in James's argument. Whereas Paul emphasized justification in the sight of God, James emphasized justification in the sight of men.

(1) The testing of his faith (v. 21*b*)

"[Wasn't Abraham] justified by works, when he had offered Isaac, his son, upon the altar?"

Abraham's faith became obvious "when he had offered Isaac, his son, upon the altar" (v. 21*b*). That's when the watching world could see the reality of his faith in God. In Genesis 22:1-2 we read, "God [tested] Abraham, and said unto him, Abraham: and he said, Behold, here I am. And he said, Take now thy son, thine only son Isaac, whom thou lovest, and get thee into the land of Moriah; and offer him there for a burnt offering upon one of the mountains which I will tell thee of."

It was approximately fifty years between God's initial call for Abraham to leave Ur of the Chaldeans and His testing of Abraham. During that time He had reiterated His covenant to Abraham: "I will make of thee a great nation, and I will bless thee, and make thy name great; and thou shalt be a blessing. And I will bless them that bless thee, and curse him that curseth thee: and in thee shall all families of the earth be blessed" (Gen. 12:2-3).

Even though Abraham was old and his wife, Sarah, was barren, he believed God for a son. When Abraham was a hundred years old God gave him Isaac. But then God asked Abraham to sacrifice his only son, a request that seemed to violate God's covenant and moral character (God forbade human sacrifice; cf. Deut. 18:10). The character and reputation of God were at stake.

Genesis 22:3-11 says, "Abraham rose up early in the morning, and saddled his ass, and took two of his young men with him, and Isaac his son, and cut the wood for the burnt offering, and rose up, and went unto the place of which God had told him. Then on the third day Abraham lifted up his eyes, and saw the place afar off. And Abraham said unto his young men, Abide ye here with the ass; and I and the lad will go yonder and worship, and come again to you.

"And Abraham took the wood of the burnt offering, and laid it upon Isaac his son; and he took the fire in his hand, and a knife; and they went both of them together. And Isaac spoke unto Abraham, his father, and said, My father: and he said, Here am I, my son. And he said, Behold the fire and the wood: but where is the lamb for a burnt offering? And Abraham said, My son, God will provide himself a lamb for a burnt offering: so they went both of them together.

"And they came to the place which God had told him of; and Abraham built an altar there, and laid the wood in order, and bound Isaac, his son, and laid him on the altar upon the wood. And Abraham stretched forth his hand, and took the knife to slay his son. And the angel of the Lord called unto him out of heaven, and said, Abraham, Abraham: and he said, Here am I."

Abraham's response of obedience demonstrated his unquestioning trust in God. He believed that if God wanted Isaac slain, He would be "able to raise him up, even from the dead" (Heb. 11:19).

Somehow God would fulfill His covenant promises. But God spared Isaac by providing a ram. Therefore Abraham called the place of sacrifice "The Lord Will Provide" (Gen. 22:14, NASB).

Two Perspectives on Justification

The Greek verb translated "justified" in James 2:21 has two meanings: "to acquit" (treat as righteous) or "to vindicate" (demonstrate as righteous). Paul emphasized the first meaning: Abraham was justified (acquitted) by faith in the sight of God (Rom. 4:3). James emphasized the second meaning: Abraham was justified (vindicated) by works in the sight of men (James 2:21). Both perspectives are correct.

(2) The perfection of his faith (v. 22)

"Seest thou how faith wrought with his works, and by works was faith made perfect?"

True salvation results in a transformed life, which results in transformed behavior. Therefore the perfection of one's faith is seen in his obedience to God.

(3) The results of his faith (v. 23)

"And the scripture was fulfilled which saith, Abraham believed God, and it was imputed unto him for righteousness; and he was called the friend of God."

The Greek word translated "fulfilled" in this context does not indicate a prophetic statement. It simply means what was true about Abraham was brought to fruition. Scripture says that Abraham was justified by faith (Gen. 15:6). The truth of that statement was demonstrated by his obedience, thereby upholding the integrity of Scripture.

Because his faith was genuine, Abraham was granted the honor and joy of being called the friend of God (2 Chron. 20:7). Jesus said to His disciples, "Ye are my friends, if ye do whatever I command you" (John 15:14). A friend of God is one who is obedient to His Word.

(4) The vindication of his faith (v. 24)

"Ye see, then, that by works a man is justified, and not by faith only."

A man's faith is vindicated by his works. That's why John Calvin wrote that faith alone justifies, but the faith that justifies is never alone (*Calvin's Commentaries*, vol. 3 [Grand Rapids: Eerdmans, 1972], pp. 285-86).

B. Rahab (v. 25)

"In like manner also was not Rahab, the harlot, justified by works, when she had received the messengers, and had sent them out another way?"

1. Her situation

Prior to the Israelites' attack upon Jericho, Joshua sent two spies into the city. They sought refuge in the home of Rahab the harlot, whose house was on the city wall. She hid the spies, lied to the king's men to protect them, then helped them escape by lowering them from her window with a cord. Before they left she said to them, "I know that the Lord has given you the land, and that your terror is fallen upon us, and that all the inhabitants of the land faint because of you. For we have heard how the Lord dried up the water of the Red Sea for you, when ye came out of Egypt; and what you did unto the two kings of the Amorites, who were on the other side of the Jordan, Sihon and Og, whom ye utterly destroyed. And as soon as we had heard these things, our heart did melt, neither did there remain any more courage in any man, because of you; for the Lord your God, He is God in heaven above, and in earth beneath" (Joshua 2:9-11).

2. Her salvation

Rahab believed in the God who had led His people out
of Egypt and defeated the Amorite kings. She believed
all she knew about God, and it was imputed to her for
righteousness. Her true faith was made manifest when
she sheltered the Israelite spies (James 2:25).

Was It Right for Rahab to Lie?

It was not right for Rahab to lie about the location of the Israelite
spies (Joshua 2:4-5). Even though she had true faith, her knowledge of God was extremely limited. She was a victim of her own
fallen nature, and her ethics were the ethics of a corrupt Canaanite
society. She did not understand the value God puts on truth, so
she turned to a sinful solution to protect herself and the spies. God
honored her faith, but her lie was unnecessary. Who knows what
God might have done if she had trusted Him rather than lying?

What Kind of Works Vindicate Faith?

In Matthew 10:38 Jesus uses the cross, an emblem of death, as an illustration of Christian commitment: "He that taketh not his cross
and followeth after me, is not worthy of me." When it comes down
to why you live and what is most valuable to you, is your faith in
God more valuable to you than everything else you hold dear?
Quite often it is in the midst of life's dire decisions that the quality
of our faith is revealed.

Abraham was willing to sacrifice his beloved son; Rahab risked her
life to shelter the Hebrew spies. Both were willing to sacrifice what
mattered most to them. They had true faith. Do you?

C. A Corpse (v. 26)

"As the body without the spirit is dead, so faith without
works is dead also."

Just as a body without life is of no value—fit only for burial
—faith without works is just as useless. Both are corrupted

and have a corrupting influence upon everyone and everything they come in contact with.

Conclusion

James calls us to examine ourselves. Do you say you believe the Bible yet not obey it? Do you claim to belong to Christ but have no desire to serve Him? Do you say you love Him but continue to love sin? Or do you loathe evil and seek righteousness? Do you choose to honor God at any cost? Is your faith useless, or is it saving faith?

Dead faith is fruitless faith; living faith produces righteous works. Abraham and Rahab proved their faith was alive when their trust in God was put to the test. God's honor was their highest goal. Let it be yours as well.

Focusing on the Facts

1. How is the phrase "our father" used in verse 21 (see p. 123)?
2. What does "justification" mean (see p. 123)?
3. What characteristics of Abraham's justification does Paul mention in Romans 4:1-25 (see pp. 123-24)?
4. Define "imputed" (see p. 125).
5. What is the sole condition of salvation (see p. 125)?
6. Why did God forgive Abraham (see p. 126)?
7. What does Abraham's statement "I and the lad will . . . come again to you" indicate about his faith (Gen. 22:5; cf. Heb. 11:19; see p. 127)?
8. What are the two perspectives on justification (see pp. 128)?
9. What were the two results of Abraham's faith (v. 23; see pp. 128-29)?
10. How did Rahab assist the Hebrew spies (Joshua 2:4-6, 15-16; see p. 129)?
11. Was it right for Rahab to lie? Explain (see p. 130).
12. In what way is dead faith similar to a corpse (v. 26; see p. 130-31)?

Pondering the Principles

1. We have seen that Abraham's faith was tested by God so it might be proved to be genuine (Gen. 22:1). But the proving of one's faith was not limited to the Old Testament. Quite often God permitted New Testament believers to experience persecution at the hands of sinful people. Read 1 Peter 1:6-9 and answer these questions:

   • How might God choose to prove the quality of your faith (vv. 6-7)?
   • What is the value of proved faith (v. 7)?
   • At what point in time will proved faith be vindicated (v. 7)?
   • What are the results of proved faith (vv. 7-9)?
   • Who is the object of true faith (v. 8)?

   Is your faith being tested now? How are you responding to that test? Remember that God hasn't promised any quick and easy paths to proved faith, but He does promise "joy inexpressible and full of glory" (v. 8).

2. Throughout Scripture Abraham is characterized as a man of faith. What a wonderful tribute to the grace of God in his life! Do those who know you see you as a person of great faith? Read the examples of faithful people listed in Hebrews 11:1–12:2. Ask God to make you an example of uncompromising faith.

Scripture Index

Topical Index

reasons to avoid, 92, 103
sinfulness of, 70, 74, 96, 98-100
socioeconomic, 65-66
spiritualizing, 94
Purity. *See* Holiness

Rahab
  lie of, 130
  salvation of, 129-30
Religion
  false, 51-54
  pure, 54-60
  true, 54-60
  useless, 53-54
Resources in Christ, 114, 119
Responsibility, the believer's, 115, 119
Revival, elements of spiritual, 30-33, 44
Riches. *See* Wealth
Royal law. *See* Law of God

Salvation
  deception about. *See* Self-deception
  equality of, 64-65, 81-82
  evaluating. *See* Self-examination
  faith and. *See* Faith
  by faith not works, 125
  impartiality of. *See* equality of
  Scripture and. *See* Scripture
  works and. *See* Faith
Sanctification. *See* Faith
Scripture
  desiring, 11-12
  flirting with, 35-43, 50-51
  hearing, 15-16, 35-43, 50-51
  immediately applying, 38-39
  nourishment by, 11-12, 15

obeying, 9-13, 16-17, 23-25, 30-62
perfection of, 40-41
preparing for, 40
reading, 17, 26
receiving, 12-26
resisting, 13-14, 20-22, 26
salvation and, 24-25
transforming power of, 14-15
Self-deception, 36-43, 49-53, 61, 108
Self-esteem, overestimation of, 104-5
Self-examination, 38-42, 44, 59, 104, 112
Simon the sorcerer, dead faith of, 117-18
Speech, limiting, 17-20, 61
Spiritual growth, Scripture and, 11-12, 15

Teachable spirit, 23-26
Teaching, limiting, 17-20
Trials, faith and, 126-28, 132. *See also* Faith

Visitation, 55-56

Wealth
  blasphemy of the rich, 91-92
  election of the rich, 83-84
  neutrality of, 75
  rich Christians, 68-69
  use of, 93-94
Wesley, Charles, on hearing Scripture, 16-17
Widows, God's concern for, 56-57, 61-62
Worldliness, avoiding, 58-59, 62
Works. *See* Faith
Wrath. *See* Anger